PRAISE FOR *WE THE INTERWOVEN*

"What a beautiful, moving, haunting collection of stories. This project, and the Bicultural Writers' Fellowship that produced it, gives me hope for what's possible in the future. By crafting the stories of their lives and sharing their struggles and accomplishments, these writers offer a generosity of spirit and the kind of insight that creates connections—with readers, with strangers, with the many different people who make up Iowa, the U.S., the world. This book is a triumph."

—Michele Morano, author of *Grammar Lessons: Translating a Life in Spain*

"*We the Interwoven* is exactly the sort of antidote we need to the kind of othering that could lead to catastrophic future outcomes. It accomplishes the vital mission of humanizing issues that are all too often relegated to abstract or overly politicized realms."

—Melissa Studdard, author of *I Ate the Cosmos for Breakfast* and host of *VIDA Voices & Views*

"*We the Interwoven* brings together different perspectives from marginalized communities whose voices we don't often hear. It gives them a face and name and a voice. This work is significant and needed."

—Ingrid Bejerman, Programming Associate, Blue Metropolis International Literary Festival

"These voices map a landscape, and in language both intimate and poetic, they reveal the many words for home."

—Inara Verzemnieks, author of *Among the Living and the Dead*

D0668718

WE the INTERWOVEN

ANTONIA RIVERA, AJLA DIZDAREVIĆ,
DAWSON DAVENPORT,
SARAH ELGATIAN, RANA HEWEZI,
HIEU PHAM, AND ANTHONY MIELKE

EDITOR ANDREA WILSON

Published by the Iowa Writers' House
www.iowawritershouse.org

The Bicultural Iowa Writers' Fellowship program
and *We the Interwoven* were funded in part by an
Art Project Grant from the Iowa Arts Council and
the National Endowment for the Arts.

First Edition

Cover art by Sayuri Sasaki Hemann

Designed by Skylar Alexander

ISBN 978-1-7324206-2-5

CONTENTS

FOREWORD

WE LIVE IN A WORLD of stories—more than seven billion personal tales are unfolding on this planet at every moment. In America, 329 million lives are linked together in the story of a country founded by people coming from afar in search of life, liberty, and happiness. For hundreds of years, that story has continued, and the cultural makeup of our country has grown and changed as people from all over the world are drawn to those ideals.

The state of Iowa, nestled in the middle of the heartland, is not well known as a home for modern immigrants, and yet this series exists as a testament otherwise. When people come to a new place, they bring their stories and add new chapters. These stories link us to a past that we must not forget, and when we share them, we live together in greater harmony.

The stories in this book, shared directly by those who lived them, might otherwise have gone untold. The Bicultural Iowa Writers' Fellowship is the only program of its kind in the state—it provides education, mentorship, and support for bicultural Americans to write their stories. The process involves deep personal work in excavating memories and unearthing truths. These stories, like the lives they reflect, are complex and nuanced.

Volume 2 of *We the Interwoven* introduces seven new voices—three fellows and four honorable-mention recipients, all with stories that explore the theme of living between two worlds. **Antonia Rivera** crossed the Mexican-American border at the age of six, and her story spans three decades of the undocumented immigrant struggle. **Dawson Davenport**, a member of the Meskwaki Nation, shares a story of inherited Native trauma manifesting in the life of a young man coming of age. **Ajla Dizdarević** shares a Bosnian-American story of cultural tradition that survived a family's migration. **Hieu Pham** explores Vietnamese-American filial debt, **Rana Hewezi** writes of an Egyptian mother's gift to her daughter, and **Anthony Mielke** discovers his hidden Puerto Rican heritage.

This book offers a rare literary experience, including cultural glossaries and language translations to help contextualize the stories. While few readers will be fluent in all of the languages, the translations promote an openness that aligns with the larger purpose of the book: engendering conversations across cultures, generations, and geographies.

America is a story still unfolding. With each new chapter, we rediscover that we are inextricably tied together, all pursuing similar hopes and dreams. Each of us has a part to play in the fabric of our country. In the end, we are all interwoven.

ANDREA WILSON
Founder, Iowa Writers' House

ACKNOWLEDGMENTS

ALL OF US involved with the Bicultural Iowa Writers' Fellowship (BIWF) and *We the Interwoven* offer our gratitude to all those who celebrated and supported our vision:

To Maggie Conroy, Inara Verzemnieks, and Hugh Ferrer for giving their time and talent to the fellowship.

To previous fellows Chuy Renteria, Melissa Palma, and Sadagat Aliyeva for continuing to be ambassadors of our program.

To all who assisted with translation, helping us honor native languages.

To the Iowa Arts Council and the National Endowment for the Arts for helping to make this program possible.

To our families and loved ones who supported us in bringing this book into the world.

To the Iowa Writers' House community for believing in our dream to champion marginalized voices and to publish books that represent a globalizing world.

ANTONIA RIVERA

ARTIST STATEMENT

I WAS BORN in 1982 in Distrito Federal, Mexico. At six years old I found refuge in the United States with my sister and my mother. Today I live in Des Moines, Iowa, with temporary protection and a work permit through the DACA policy—Deferred Action for Childhood Arrivals. I am what many refer to as a "Dreamer." At almost forty years old, I am noticeably older than the rest of the DACA population in Iowa—I have been undocumented for longer than many of them have been alive.

I live in an eternal state of survival, but it is in Iowa that I've finally had a chance to rest and lay down roots, raise my daughter, and find peace. Iowa is my safe haven, a place where I found a vibrant immigrant community to become part of. It is Iowa that allows me to finally explore my identity.

When I started this project, I had no idea that I would end up sharing my undocumented story. For the first couple of months, I was stuck trying to figure out what my culture was. How could I write about my identity when I felt so displaced, ni de aquí ni de allí, *from neither here nor there? I was born in Mexico, but I am not a real Mexican. My culture is not mariachis or margaritas. My culture is the undocu-culture of my undocumented experience in the United States. I am part of the 1.5 generation, stuck between the immigrants who migrated as adults and the children born in the United States.*

So, I wrote bits and pieces about my experience and about Iowa, all mostly abstract work, until I realized it was time to share my real story. It was difficult and emotionally draining, but through it all, writing has been my therapy, my undocu-joy, my freedom, and my strength. I realized that I am not ready to give up. I do not want my daughter to have to worry about me how I worry about my mother. I refuse to die without being free. Sharing my story may have consequences, but I want to be able to look into the future owning every moment of my past. I hope that everyone walks away from reading my piece with new perspective.

I, ANTONIA:
AN UNDOCUMENTED STORY

ANTONIA RIVERA
IN COLLABORATION WITH ANDREA WILSON

THE DAUGHTER
1982
DISTRITO FEDERAL, MEXICO

I WAS BORN the great-granddaughter of Ma Tola and Ninfa, granddaughter of Mama Nina, daughter of Maria. I was a product of the Mexican Revolution, a cross between the light skin and hazel eyes of my father's mother, Crecencia, and the light skin and caramel eyes of my maternal grandmother, Mama Nina. I was a fusion between Estado de Mexico and Oaxaca.

The origin of the blood running through my veins was irrelevant to me: careless child, spoiled child, daughter of the city, daughter of the smog, daughter throwing tantrums, playing with her dolls, rejecting her mother's homemade feasts and *agua fresca*. I had no worries, except when I had to act like a lady, wearing a perfectly ironed dress, white socks with ruffles, shiny black *zapatos de charol*, part of a traditional nuclear family. With a straight back and elbows off the table, I sat, learning to cut my steak with a fork and a knife, learning to say please and thank you, trying desperately to throw away my mother's homemade feast, unable to understand why a proper meal was necessary when I could survive on candy. But even when I had to mind my manners, I was a daughter with a free heart.

THE WITNESS
1986-1988
DISTRITO FEDERAL, MEXICO

I BEGAN TO KNOW WORRY. The 1985 earthquake had crumbled the city. Our house survived, but it trembled with tension. I was suddenly a sister and not the only child. In a city and a country full of machismo, men ruled.

My mother was bigger than the sun. In my father's presence, she was light. I used to watch her every move with admiration. My father would demand food; she would talk back and give it to the dog. He would forbid her to get a job; she would go sew at the local garment factory while he was at work. She sewed in silence until he found out. In fury, he dragged her home by her long locks of ebony hair. In master rebellion style, she cut it up to her shoulders. I watched in awe. The day he threw her baby on the couch, took off his belt, and burst open her sister's lip, she realized he was a danger to not just her but to those around her, and she decided to leave.

She went to the police. He spent a night in jail and came home more angry. She asked if she could get a divorce. They told her he had to agree. They told her she was his property.

Everything we had was tied to him. The Mexican laws favored him. She was trapped.

I watched it all with wide eyes, afraid for her life.

We began to plan an escape. We knew we had to leave Mexico, at least for a while. Anywhere we went in Mexico, he could find us, he could call the police, and as his property, she would be returned. The U.S. was the closest place where he had no legal power over us.

My mother and I started collecting things—her favorite clothes, my little sister's and my favorite toys, birth certificates, immunization records—and stowing them with trusted neighbors and friends to keep them until we returned. Over six months, little by little, we organized the most important things in our life and hid them away.

Everything had to be planned in advance. We couldn't stay anywhere for too long, and we couldn't talk to people. We knew he would come after us, so we calculated how fast he could follow us and how long we could stay in one place. A work day was eight hours. My mom's hometown was five hours away by bus, and from there we would wait until our secret network told us he found out we were gone.

The bus trip to Tijuana took almost a week. Once we were on

4

the bus, he wouldn't know our route. When the bus dropped us off, we would get a motel room and plan our escape to California, the place where he would no longer have power over us.

THE FUGITIVE
1988
MEXICAN-AMERICAN BORDER

I SAT AT A RESTAURANT eating my last Mexican street taco. It was probably *lengua*, because that was my favorite.

"Come tacos. Come mucho, porque si nos agarran, no nos van a dar de comer. Eat tacos, eat many, because if they catch us, they are not going to give us anything to eat," the scrawny man shoving tacos into his mouth advised me. He had been detained before, and he knew that even if it was only a night in a holding cell, we would be hungry. I knew then, whether I made it without spending a night in jail or not, I was going to start thinking like an outlaw. Like an adventurer.

We didn't cross the river because it was too dangerous for kids. Instead our plan was to walk across the land, dry, dusty *tierra* with bushes and nothing else; then through a sewer; and then over a small chain-link fence. They said when we saw the road, we would know we were in *El Norte.*

I was not afraid. I was saving my mother, and this was an adventure.

At one point, we waited in bushes for the border patrol to make their rounds and pass by. At the first sight of the blaring helicopter lights, the taco man panicked and rushed out from the bushes that sheltered me. Other people ran too. I couldn't see anything from the bushes, but someone whispered, "They got them." He would have to spend a night in jail, they said, and then he would be released. But I waited, silently, patiently.

When it was time, I walked through the sewers and through a little hole in the barely-taller-than-me, barbed-wire, chain-link fence that separated Mexico from the United States. Then a lady appeared with *mole, pozole, pastel,* homemade tortillas, and grapes, lots of grapes. In a hut on the side of the border, I ate a meal fit for a king. She did not see me as a criminal but as a fugitive traveling through a compassionate underground railroad on my way to safety. I felt like a hero saving my mother. I also felt like a tourist on my way to Disneyland, good people just passing through, meaning no harm. We would be safe there—America would be my safe haven.

THE GROWN-UP
1988-1989
ANAHEIM, CALIFORNIA

IN MEXICO, when we dreamed about the US, we dreamed about Disneyland. But in the city of Disneyland, I lived among stacked rows of sleeping bodies covering the brown carpet of our tiny apartment.

La Temple was a street embedded in the outskirts of Anaheim. Our first apartment had one bedroom with twenty to twenty-five people sleeping in the living room, mostly men. They would talk about coming to work the jobs that Americans would no longer do. They talked about how they almost had enough money to go back to Mexico, to build their own homes and start their own businesses, to go back to their children and their wives.

They loved their Mexico. They said they would never trade it for *El Norte*, where they lived like rats, piled one on top of the other, eating fake hamburgers instead of the homemade meals their mamas and wives would cook for them back home. But there were jobs here, jobs that people wanted to pay them to do.

I was not sure if I wanted to go home, but I used to wonder when our journey would end. When would we get a bed? When would we stop moving? I used to dress up my baby sister like a doll and wonder why she got to be treated like a child, why she got toys, why she kissed my mom without a worry in the world.

Meanwhile, my father came after us. As the man of the house and a homeowner with a job, he qualified for a tourist visa, one my mother never could have gotten without his permission. He found out through the grapevine where we were—one of my mom's relatives finally told him. He came to the apartment. My mother panicked but held her ground and spoke to him through the doorway. I was afraid, but I knew the men of La Temple, my uncles, would protect us. He begged and pleaded, saying he loved her and wanted her to come home. She told him she would not go and that she wanted a divorce. He said he would never give it to her. Then he returned to Mexico.

I was a child, except I wasn't. Because I learned English more quickly than the adults, I was the one they went to. For the men of La Temple, I became a lawyer, doctor, translator, landlord, banker, parent, and negotiator. I approved or disapproved of the contracts for a new apartment. I went with them to immigration court. I translated immigration papers for them. Because I was the interpreter, I would make the final decision. I looked grown men in the eye and gave them my recommendations, told them where to sign, what to do.

I saw things. I read things. Things children were not supposed to worry about.

Women were rare in La Temple. Those women who did come left their kids back home with their grandparents. Like the men, they came over on a short business trip, to work temporarily before going home, maybe even for the thrill of the adventure.

My mother, my baby sister, and I were different. Before I came to Anaheim, I told my mother I was not going to stay with my grandmother in Mexico. I was not going to be a child left behind and forgotten. We were in America not in search of a better life for our family back in Mexico but in search of a place where we could stay together and be safe.

There were no other kids in La Temple besides me and my baby sister. Kids typically did not come in those days. I felt sorry for the kids left home with their mothers or grandmothers in Mexico. I was starting to see many of the men of La Temple fall in love with American girlfriends. I was starting to see them forget their families back home.

The only kids I knew were at school. Most of them were white, and the few who were not white were first- or second-generation Americans. Many of their parents were remnants from the Bracero

Program, which invited Mexicans to come as seasonal workers while American men were off at war or at work. Even though the program ended in the 1960s, the jobs were still being offered—by farmers, by factories, by everyone. We were the workforce for those jobs at the bottom.

As a child, you hear everything. When I went along to translate, I would hear the adults talking about how the Americans wanted more workers. They said we were hard workers, that we didn't complain and weren't lazy. The men were always working two or three jobs. There was no overtime, but two jobs meant twice the money.

People didn't talk about getting citizenship back then. The people of La Temple always wanted to go home to Mexico. Meanwhile, the parents of my friends at school were either born here or were legalizing their status through Ronald Reagan's 1986 amnesty. The program was created for adults who came before January 1, 1982, and their relatives. It was so easy to receive the amnesty that many people did not worry about applying for it even if they qualified. My mom didn't apply because we were planning on going back home someday, when my father would hopefully grant her a divorce and we could return safely.

No one was nervous about policy. The immigration laws seemed to be getting more and more favorable. I watched George H. W. Bush sign a bill increasing the number of visas on the same small TV where we watched *Looney Tunes* and *The Three Stooges*.

Every day at school, I placed a hand over my heart and recited the Pledge of Allegiance with a proud voice. With a proud voice, I sang

My country, 'tis of thee
Sweet land of liberty . . .
and
This land is your land,
This land is my land . . .

THE SILENT ONE
1990
SANTA ANA, CALIFORNIA

I MOVED, but I was still in California and beginning to wonder if our temporary stay wasn't so temporary.

Even though I was a child, I understood something was starting to change. I was seeing more women like my mother. Women were starting to come in bigger numbers, and they had children with them.

My new school had a lot of immigrant kids, and more were coming all the time. These kids looked different. Their clothes were different. They were not only Mexican, they were also Central American, mainly Salvadoran and Guatemalan. Many had been through terrible things in their countries. The adults said they were escaping violence. I heard that the law Bush signed gave a lot of them the chance to come.

I saw those kids get bullied by U.S.-born Mexican kids. It scared me to see them treated like that. They didn't speak English, and they couldn't defend themselves with words.

The new kids were put into ESL (English as a Second Language), a program that had not existed at the first school I attended because there were not many immigrants. When I arrived at my new school, I was in the regular classes at first, mostly with Mexican-American kids who spoke English. I heard the way they talked about the ESL kids. They made fun of the way they talked and the food they ate. They made fun of everything.

A few weeks after arriving, the teachers told me that because English was not my first language, I would be put into ESL. I had learned English at my first school, and I didn't want to be taken out of the regular English and math classes. But most of all, I didn't want to be bullied.

When my teachers and my mother did not listen to my desperate requests to be taken out of ESL, I decided not to give them another option. I took the ESL workbook that we were going to learn for the year and finished it on my own. One day, I went to my teacher with

9

the finished book. I gave it to her and told her I was done. As we used to say, there were no ifs, buts, or coconuts. Without officially graduating from the ESL program, I was released back into the regular classes.

It was then that I decided to take a personal oath of silence. I was not going to talk to kids, only to teachers. I stopped making friends. If they tried to talk to me in class, I buried my face in books.

I studied when the other kids played. I did my work. I answered the teacher's questions. I read books. I was the teacher's pet. The awards started pouring in. Perfect Attendance. Outstanding Student.

At the same time I was watching the immigrant kids get treated as second-class citizens, I began to learn about the Holocaust. Many of my teachers were children of Holocaust survivors. Some of those survivors came to speak at an assembly and in our classes. I saw the numbers permanently inked on their skin. I saw black-and-white videos of people being rounded up and put in gas chambers. I saw Nazis marching in a perfectly formed swastika. I saw advertisements and media clips that blamed the Jews for everything that was bad.

The same school year, we watched footage of the Berlin Wall coming down, a barrier that separated families on two sides of a border. I also read *The Diary of Anne Frank*. The ESL classes made it very clear—immigrants were seen as a problem, as "those people." I began to wonder: Would those immigrant kids and I become like Anne?

Maybe America wasn't my safe haven after all.

THE CRIMINAL
1993-1996
SANTA ANA AND ANAHEIM, CALIFORNIA

HE CALLED ME a criminal.

He was so handsome, he was so charming, and he broke my heart. "Criminals. Criminals. Criminals." He kept saying it.

Bill Clinton was the first man I heard equate the idea of the border with safety, as if Americans needed to be protected from people like me. He made the case for building a wall and increasing patrols along the border in Operations Safeguard and Hold the Line.

He talked about protecting American children. But I was a child in need of protection, too. Why was he criminalizing me?

He talked about the war on drugs as if everyone who crossed the border were a drug dealer. But I had never seen drugs before in my life. I never saw the men from La Temple do drugs. They would drink, but there were no drugs. I went to a Mexican school and I never saw drugs. Where were these drugs he was talking about?

Did he not realize that every word he said was a dagger to my eleven-year-old heart? Did he not realize that he was caging me in and laying a foundation for exclusion from the life, liberty, and pursuit of happiness that I was learning about in my history books?

He announced they would be building a border wall, a steel chain-link fence. It would be built in pieces and phases, but it was clear that the main crossing where we came through, the area between Tijuana and San Diego, would be part of the first phase, and fence would run along the Rio Grande.

Chaos, confusion, and bewilderment set in among those who had taken the amnesty for granted. Three million people had applied and received amnesty, but the window had closed and now a wall was going up. We had kept in touch with our old friends from Anaheim, and everyone was worried. It became normal to come home and hear stories about people who were caught at the border, fingerprinted, and given orders to never attempt to cross again. They were told they would be incarcerated, and not just for a night in a holding cell. Now women and men and children were going to a real jail where they were booked and processed as criminals. This went on their record as a deportation, which meant they couldn't come back to the U.S. for many years or even for life, depending on the circumstances of their case. It became normal to hear stories of INS, *la migra*, in our backyard, like at Jax, our local market. The world we were living in became much more dangerous for all of us.

The men we knew had to make a choice: continue living as seasonal workers without work permits and risk incarceration, deportation, and an official record when they went home to visit, or stay in the U.S. and completely give up their lives in their home country.

Even though the law changed, the job opportunities did not. Employers wanted them to stay, wanted their labor. Many of them had land and houses back in Mexico where they planned to visit and eventually retire. If they chose to stay, they would never see their families, because the border was too much of a risk now. But they would have money to send back to Mexico, *remesas,* so they could feed their mothers, wives, and children. Even the minimum wage in the U.S. was four times the wages at home.

The changes to immigration policy meant that anyone staying in the U.S. as undocumented now risked not just deportation but a criminal record. Anyone who had ever stayed undocumented for more than 180 days was subject to the ban. This was our situation—my mother, my sister, and I. We did not have papers to be here, and the laws changing meant our lives were in danger. When they began to build the wall, my mother went to notaries and lawyers to see about getting amnesty. But she didn't qualify, and by that point the amnesty had closed anyway.

There was no mention of child immigrants in the media—everything was about men and criminals—but I had come here and I was a little girl, not a man. Somehow I knew what they were saying would affect all of us, even my little sister who was just a baby. I also knew one day I would be an adult, and they would be looking for me.

Once they built the border wall, our move was no longer temporary. My father hadn't agreed to give my mother the divorce, and she would be his property if we went back. The stories of the harshness at the border, of the jails, continued to come through. Everyone was scared because if you returned after a deportation order, it would be on your record forever. If you had a criminal record, you would never qualify for amnesty. Good people were getting criminal records. They would go home to see their families, and when they came back to do the seasonal work, they were jailed along with criminals and thieves. Our friends would tell us, "They take your clothes and check for drugs, they touch you."

The border had become a business. Like in the years of Prohibition, when alcohol prices went up because it was illegal, the same thing happened with crossing the border. Before, having a *pollero* or a coyote was optional, and if you needed one, it was cheap. Now things were different. You couldn't cross the border just anywhere. You needed to go over a river, dig a hole, or go through the desert, all the most dangerous places. The coyotes knew the border, the fence and the physical areas where you could cross, and now their prices were between $3,000 and $5,000 dollars per person, plus another $3,000 to $5,000 if you were Central American.

Once I knew we were staying for good, the only other thing I knew was that I had to prove I was not who they said I was.

THE HONORS STUDENT
1993-1998
SANTA ANA AND ANAHEIM, CALIFORNIA

I LOVED SCHOOL, and I made friends with other kids who loved it too. I was at the top of my class, and by the time I was in seventh grade, I was taking advanced math and English classes. In algebra, I discovered my love for solving problems. In English classes, I was assigned advanced reading and writing, and I realized how much I loved both.

My teachers saw I was exceeding the requirements and started to suggest extracurricular activities for me to learn and grow even more. I joined an after-school program for Future Scientists and Engineers of America, where college students helped us run experiments. We built bridges or tested how water reacted to certain chemicals and forces, and I decided I would become an engineer when I went to college.

I also joined the band and played the clarinet. I loved music and performing, and the band room was my home away from home. We were all equals in the band room—it offered all of us a place where we belonged.

In middle school, our concert band began to travel for performances, and we went to see the Los Angeles Philharmonic. In high school, our marching band performed at Disneyland. I was living the American High School Dream. Life had given me so many opportunities, had helped me achieve so many successes.

We weren't practicing Catholics, but we always had our faith. Every night before I went to bed, I said my prayers with a grateful heart:

Ángel de mi guarda,
Dulce compañía, no me desampares
Ni de noche, ni de día
No me dejes sola
Que me perdería

My guardian angel
Sweet company, don't leave me
Night or day
Don't leave me alone
I will be lost.

But then one day I was notified that my schedule was going to change. Once again, I was going to be taken out of my advanced English and math classes to be put into ESL. I had been in classes with native English speakers my whole life, except for that brief moment when I had been placed in ESL in first grade.

"You never tested out of the ESL program in first grade. You have to take a language proficiency test. So now state law is mandating that you be put in ESL classes until the state tests everyone toward the end of the first quarter," I was told. My heart sank. I was going to miss weeks of work in my advanced classes.

"Hello. My. Name. Is," the teacher said slowly. "Put. Your. Name. In. The. Book. The. *Libro*. What. Is. Your. Name. *Nombre*," she said, talking to us like we were one-year-olds. She had no

14

control over her students. The Hispanic teenagers would talk to her using words that had double meanings in Spanish and we would all laugh, even the Middle Eastern and Asian kids who did not speak English or Spanish but who knew this class was a joke. The teacher would read from the textbook for ten minutes and then sit down, never checking to see if anyone needed help. Everyone would finish their work in a few minutes and talk for the rest of the class.

She was "teaching" us how to say *he, she, they, the, but*—words I had learned in first grade. A lot of my classmates told me that the math was even easier. In their countries, they were taking algebra and geometry in sixth grade or before. But once they got to the United States, they were put in remedial courses because they did not speak English. We were currently learning how to add and subtract, and yet I had learned algebra the summer after sixth grade!

I felt so angry at the whole situation. None of us deserved this treatment, not even the teacher. I had to stay in ESL until I tested out few weeks later and went back to my dreamlike life.

THE ONE HIDING A SECRET
1998-1999
ANAHEIM, CALIFORNIA

THROUGHOUT HIGH SCHOOL, my status as undocumented didn't deter me from reaching for the stars. I was an honors student, an athlete, a band student, and a future engineer—I felt like the all-American high school student with the world in front of me. My friends and I were always talking about our future. We were driven, passionate, and excited for what was to come.

But in eleventh grade, I began to realize my opportunities were coming to an end.

I was the kind of student who wanted to take advantage of every prospect that came my way. That year, the librarian told me about an opportunity to be a student worker at the front office during summer school. It paid $12 to $15 an hour, but more than the money, I wanted to know what work felt like, what it was like to be an adult. I filled out the paperwork and started the job, but when

15

it came time to get my first check, they asked for my Social Security number. I didn't have one, and I was so ashamed that I kept going to work the entire summer without ever asking about getting paid.

More opportunities continued to pass me by. That same year, Anaheim had a sister city in Mito, Japan, and students were offered a chance to visit the school there. I wanted to go, but I knew I needed an American passport to come back.

Eleventh grade is when all of the applications come to a high schooler. One day my counselor told me, "Antonia, I think you should apply for this Bill Gates scholarship. I think you have a real chance of getting it." I read all of the materials and discovered it was a full-ride scholarship to the college or university of my choice. I met all of the requirements and had a solid personal statement. Then I looked at the final checklist: "Applicants must be legal permanent residents."

My heart was broken. That was when I started to realize that my status was going to be a roadblock to my future. Without a Social Security number and permanent residency, I would not able to apply for any form of financial support. My mom had a stable job, but she had two more daughters and money was tight. She was working third shift and even getting some raises, but it was just enough to pay for what we needed to live, not for college tuition.

I didn't know how I was going to go to college without scholarships. I didn't want to work without a Social Security number—I wanted to do things the right way. I had hoped the laws would change and there would be an opportunity for amnesty by the time I graduated from university. My plan was to fund my college education with scholarships and work legally after getting my degree. Now my future was up in the air.

I did more research, desperate to find out what was possible. I discovered more bad news. The state of California was going to charge me out-of-state tuition. As a nonresident, they would allow me to go to college or university, but I would pay the same as someone from another state.

Slowly I began to sink to the background. My friends started getting their driver's licenses and taking the AP exams for college. I couldn't get a license because you needed a Social Security card to get one. I couldn't get an ID, either, and you needed one of those to take the exams. While I was a student, they always accepted my school ID, but I was realizing that in the real world, you needed a real ID.

Everywhere I looked, I didn't qualify for things. I was outside the system. There was no place for me, yet I was there.

While all of this was happening, I suffered in secret. No one knew I was undocumented—in my mind, I wore the scarlet letter underneath the Mexican *nopal* on my forehead. No one ever imagined that the honors kid could be without papers.

One day, I stood in front of my AP English class and read a poem called "Richard Cory" by Edwin Arlington Robinson. The poem is about a rich man everyone thinks has the perfect life until one day he kills himself. I shared my theories about the poem with my classmates: "The reader knows there is a reason underneath. Sometimes people seem like they live a perfect life, but it's just a façade covering up the pain inside."

I felt like Richard Cory—I had been the perfect student. I got good grades, I participated, I volunteered, I had done everything that had been asked of me. That was my wealth. But inside, I felt like my life was ending and I was about to die.

UC Irvine had an exclusive outreach program, and the summer between my junior and senior year, I applied and was chosen. As part of the program, I had to start working on my personal statement for college applications. It was an essay about why you wanted to go to college.

I imagined that five years out of high school, I would have my bachelor's degree in biomedical engineering with a minor in French. My heart would be filled from working at the university labs combined with top-notch admission to summer internships and study-abroad experiences. I would be reimagining technology as a working professional. I would come back as a MAES (Mexican-American Engineers and Scientists) mentor and be highlighted at their annual symposium, which I had been attending as a high schooler. Now, I would be the keynote speaker, thanking MAES for investing in our youth, for helping us to dream that anything was possible with an education and that nothing could get in the way if we had determination.

The room would roar with claps, stomps, and whistles. Some would start twirling their white napkins like lassos. I would thank the audience and take my seat next to legends like José Hernández, a Mexican-American NASA astronaut who worked his way out of the crop fields of California. He had given a speech at one of the symposiums I had attended, inspiring me to persevere so I might one day take the stage.

I wasn't ready to give up on this vision for my life, but I was starting to fear it would never come true.

THE HIGH SCHOOL SENIOR
1999-2000
ANAHEIM, CALIFORNIA; STONE PARK, ILLINOIS; GRAND CANYON, ARIZONA

SENIOR YEAR is a year of lasts. That fall, I ran my last cross country meet. I played my last marching band competition. I cheered on the team at our last football game. But at the same time, there was a dark cloud over me. My time was almost up, and soon my secret would be revealed. I felt like Cinderella, praying that the clock would never strike midnight or that I could make a quiet exit.

In October, we found out my uncle and his family were going to move to Chicago. When he told my mother the news, he offered to bring us with him. She had just bought a house, the first house she'd ever owned, bought with her own money that she made working third shift all those years at a hanger factory. But my mother had recently given birth to my third sister and had split with the father. Now with two young daughters, the idea of being without her siblings was overwhelming. We had never lived away from our family.

She had just signed the escrow papers, and there was a three-day clause before the contract was official. I realized this was my chance for a quiet exit. If I moved to Chicago, my friends wouldn't realize I wasn't going to college after graduation. They wouldn't see my undocumented shame.

We decided to go.

Over the next few weeks, I said my goodbyes. I waved goodbye to the empty basketball courts from sixth grade, the best year of my life, when I had Mrs. McMillan's caramel candies. I waved goodbye to the sweaty locker room, to the track and field, to the lunch tables where I sat with friends every day. I waved goodbye to Cook Auditorium where I took in the applause after every performance, to the grand white building with classrooms where I stressed over the strict honors curriculum, to the stage where we had all the pep rallies. I said goodbye to Glover Stadium, the place where I played my clarinet and the drums for football games and marching band competitions. It was also the place where I would have sat among my teachers and friends on the final day of my high school career, waiting for the moment I had looked forward to my entire life: walking across the stage to receive my diploma. Instead, my shame was causing me to miss it all.

On top of that, it turned out that being a transfer student wasn't at all how I thought it would be.

My red Converse shoes were no match for the ice-covered sidewalks outside Proviso West High School in the Chicago suburbs. It was my first time in the Midwest. I felt like a penguin as I walked up to the school.

As I finally reached the front door, I was shocked to see a metal detector and students using security cards to enter. "Welcome!" one of the security guards with a yellow jacket greeted me. I had never imagined going to school under so much surveillance. Inside, there were TV security screens everywhere and yellow-jacketed guards at every exit.

I expected see mostly white kids because it was the Midwest, so I was surprised when the counselor introduced me to two Mexican girls.

"I want you to show Antonia around and make her feel welcome," she told them. I wondered why she was only introducing me to Mexican girls—they were not even in any of my classes, and I wanted to meet someone I would be with every day. I had missed a lot of school due to the move and finals were in a couple of weeks, so I was hoping to meet people from my classes who could help me catch up.

There were no AP classes equivalent to the ones I was taking in Anaheim, so the counselor put me in the existing honors classes. As the first class began, I realized things were going to be even more different here than I'd thought.

"Can anyone answer?" asked the teacher. Everyone kept talking, some even with their backs to the front of the room. "Turn around! Stop talking!" she yelled.

"No," one of the kids said. I was shocked. I could not believe their audacity, and I was also confused. This was an honors class. Why were the honors kids acting up?

I went to lunch.

"Come sit with us," the girls I met in the counselor's office said. Within minutes, a plastic dish of mayo ketchup flew across the cafeteria and splattered all over a group of African Americans. Then milk cartons were thrown back from the other side. Suddenly a battle between the Mexicans and the African Americans broke out, girls and boys, pulling hair, calling names, throwing punches. This was no funny little food fight like we used to have when I was younger where we would end up giggling. This was gang war. Minutes later, yellow jackets buzzed by to break things up, their whistles piercing the air.

What I had gotten myself into? In my high school in California, we had our different groups—the jocks, the punks, the band students, the ESL kids—and it was easy to move from one cafeteria table to the next. There wasn't this kind of tension. There wasn't this racial divide, this war.

I was scared to go to school. I felt like I was in a prison. I swiped my card, and I kept to myself. I stayed in the empty band room, the only place I felt safe. I missed my friends, my old band, my old band room.

I realized that I wanted to go back. I wanted to finish strong. I wanted to graduate with my friends. I decided to go back to Anaheim to finish school.

The year before, my father had come to the United States. He had a visitor visa and had started coming to visit. He said he wanted to make things right with my sister and me, although my mom had not forgiven him. By the time of these visits, he had stopped drinking and was living a quiet life. People who didn't know about his past would describe him as funny, gentle, and willing to help. I considered these changes with hesitation—I still held the memories of when we left and what we lived through. At the same time, I could see he was a different man than the one I remembered and the one my mother told me about. And although my mother knew he would never be a good husband to her, she was willing to give him the opportunity to be a father.

When I decided to go back to California, he offered to overstay his visa and to be my father for the first time since we had left him in Mexico. I felt like I hardly knew him, but with so many senior events coming up, I wanted to go back as soon as possible. We made the arrangements and I flew home.

I was thrilled to be back with my friends, back with the band, back in my favorite AP classes. I especially liked AP bio, the class that got to go on field trips. We went to the most beautiful parts of the Western United States, like the River Walk in San Antonio, the Space Needle in Seattle, and the hiking trails in Yosemite.

One day I was on the bus, enjoying the scenery as we cruised toward the Grand Canyon. Out of nowhere, a boy turned to me. He was not my close friend, but I knew who he was—the student-body president, the football star, the smartest kid in our class, the kid who would become valedictorian.

"I don't have papers," he said.

I was shocked, as if I had jumped into cold water. I never expected another kid to have the same problem as me, to be undocumented.

We were supposed to explore the different layers of a big hole in Arizona that had formed over millennia of existence. Instead, I discovered him and our shared displacement. While everyone else on that bus was expected to go to college, we knew we might not be able to.

"What are you going to do after we graduate?" I asked.

"I am going to run away, far away, where no one can ever find me," he said. He looked determined.

My heart sank deeper than the Grand Canyon. He was fighting a deportation order. I didn't understand, I thought those orders were only for adults, and I'd never met a kid fighting one.

We sat on the bus and spoke quietly to each other, two people without a future.

THE GRADUATE
2000
ANAHEIM, CALIFORNIA

I ARRIVED at Disneyland with my class, determined to leave my worries behind. The most magical place in the world was only down the street from my home but might as well have been on another planet, a luxury kids like me could not normally afford. Tonight was an exception—it was grad night and the park would be open after hours. We arrived, determined to celebrate all the hard work and sacrifices that it took to get here. We would celebrate together and create one last memory as the class of 2000.

The night was enchanted. Mickey Mouse was our master of ceremonies. There was food, and there were DJs from local radio stations. The park was full of students from across California. The lines were so long that we rode the kiddie rides, turning circles on teacups, riding carts over wooden railroads, and giggling through It's a Small World. As we walked from one area to another, we were transported into another world, full of fairy dust and twinkling lights, laughs and whimsical rides. We were graduating high school, and it was our last moment of being kids. I was having so much fun that I didn't notice the time going by until I looked up at the sky and saw the glimmer of dawn.

It was time to say goodbye to Mickey Mouse and to our youth. It was time to go graduate into adulthood. We jumped back on the bus. We had to make it back to Glover Stadium for the ceremony practice, and then we would walk the stage for real in our caps and gowns, moving our tassels to signify the completion of our American high school experience.

I sat at the front, part of the top two percent of the class, proudly wearing all my sashes, ribbons, and pins, happy that I got to sit next to my best friends. Although the ceremony was two hours long, it happened all too fast. With the last note of "Pomp and Circumstance," I felt like I was Cinderella and the clock had struck midnight.

My college acceptance letter was in the drawer, but without documentation to apply as an in-state student or for scholarships, I couldn't afford to go—that dream was impossible. Without a work permit, I couldn't even legally be a contributing member of society. I accepted my fate—it was time to enter the next phase of my life, a life without mentors and guardians, a life without legal status, a life where I would be an adult and in the same category as all the other immigrants. I would be the same as the men from La Temple—even with my diploma in hand, everything I had done in high school would disappear.

THE WORKER
2000-2002
STONE PARK, ILLINOIS

I MOVED BACK to my mother's house near Chicago. With no plan, I joined the labor force with my fellow immigrants. I started working odd jobs through temp agencies, work that undocumented people could do in factories and plants. For eight hours a day, I put the lid on the popcorn can, I folded the right edge of the pamphlet, I put the screw in the bag, I put the cap on the shampoo bottle.

In working with other undocumented immigrants, I learned that Chicago had a system to help us survive. The people at the factories told me about something called a *Matrícula Consular*. It was an ID for Mexican nationals that the city had voted to accept as a form of identification. With it, I could get a library card and a checking account.

I decided to take a semester of night classes at Triton, a community college. The single scholarship I had received when I graduated high school was a local one for a thousand dollars that did not have a residency requirement, and it would cover my tuition for a semester. I missed school, and even though community college had not been my original plan, I was glad to do anything that used my brain for more than screwing on a shampoo cap. I signed up for calculus, chemistry, and English classes, and when they asked for my major, I checked the box for engineering. I couldn't get a bachelor's degree there, but I could do my prerequisites and maybe transfer to a university one day if the laws changed.

My classmates were nontraditional students. Many of them already had a college education and were going back to school. Many were parents with children. There were also a lot of Polish immigrants who were trying to learn English.

During this time, I joined the youth group at my church. It was led by the Hispanic ministry and part of a youth network all around Chicago. I was lonely and looking for something to be part of. They introduced me to other groups where I met young, first-generation immigrants. Many of them were struggling with drugs and alcohol. Most were born in Mexico and came here to work and send money home to their families, but their lives were so lonely. Unlike the men from La Temple, these kids were supporting the generation above them as well as their siblings. They were paying for their little brothers' school books and their little sisters' shoes back home, where no one understood how hard their lives were. Their families believed that the U.S. was the land of money and that life was so much better here.

Migration was not beautiful for us. We were all struggling in one way or another, trying to fit in and make ends meet. We would sing and cook for each other and tell our stories. I felt such a connection with their tales. I understood their sadness, and I wanted to tell them that we were all in this together, and that no matter how deep they had fallen, they could always get up.

After a while, I became a youth group leader. One night, I stood up to share my story. *"Hola, yo soy Antonia Rivera. Tengo diecinueve años, y soy una líder. Yo tampoco tengo papeles.* Hello, my name is Antonia Rivera. I'm nineteen years old, and I'm a leader. I also don't have papers." That was when I started sharing my undocumented story. I learned that it could help people open up about their own situations.

When we told our stories, we were supposed to share our goals and dreams. I shared that my dream was to go back to school. So many of them still had to get their GEDs, still had to learn the language. "You have to go back, Antonia," they would say. *"Tu que puedes, ve a la escuela. Hazlo por nosotros.* You can do it, go to school. Do it for us."

One day the phone rang. It was Mr. Ameele, my former band teacher, calling to tell me that a new law passed in California. AB 540 meant I could get in-state tuition. I had already applied to UC Irvine and been accepted.

My pride, my determination as a high schooler that I would never be the kind of immigrant who worked without papers, was gone. I just wanted my education, my chance to be an engineer, to have a future. I wanted my dream back.

THE COLLEGIATE
2002
IRVINE, CALIFORNIA

I STARTED COLLEGE in Irvine, a city built in the 1970s, so new that it looked like a utopia. Every square inch was part of a master plan for the future. But it was no utopia for me. Although there was a law that allowed me to attend college with in-state tuition, my school was not ready for me. I had to fight for everything.

I had to explain why I did not have a state ID over and over again. I had a *Matrícula Consular*—an ID given to Mexican nationals living outside of Mexico that was accepted in many places in Chicago. It was even accepted for flying on a plane. But in California, no one knew what a *Matrícula* was.

"Please, I go to this school. I need to check out this book."

"This is not a valid ID card. You need to show me a California driver's license," the librarian insisted.

"I don't have a California ID card," I said, desperately hoping this woman would help me.

"Why don't you just go to the DMV and get one?" she asked, as if anyone could just walk up to the DMV and get a driver's license.

I left without the books I needed for my courses.

"You can't come in," the doorman said. We were out celebrating a birthday.

"Why?" I asked.

"I have to scan your ID. My machine does not recognize this," he said, pointing at my *Matrícula*.

"Antonia, it's okay, we don't have to stay," said my friends.

I wished the world would swallow me whole. I wished I were invisible.

"I would have let you go, but I'm training him," the policeman said.

My original plan was to wait until I was legalized to start driving, but I couldn't afford to live in Irvine, and the farther I worked and lived away from school, the less practical riding the bus had become. Public transportation did not offer twenty-four-hour service, and the distances were too far to walk. I had to learn to drive and borrow my dad's car without a license.

I went into convulsions whenever I noticed headlights behind my car. My whole body would shake. My foot would hit the brake uncontrollably. Please go away. Please, please. Go. Go away. Go. Fear like that, it paralyzes you. You hold your breath with so much intensity it feels as if the blood is oozing out of your veins, leaving your brain limp and lifeless. When the police drove behind me, even if they were not approaching me, I started to panic. Was my brake light broken? Was the car properly registered? Was I going too fast or too slow? Would the police decide to read my license plate without a reason? Today it was the taillight.

"Get out and sit on the curb," said the trainee. He began to search the back seat. "Where are the drugs?" he demanded. "I can't find any drugs."

"Just give her a ticket," the first policeman said, stopping him from searching. The trainee went to protest, but the officer interrupted, "She doesn't have a driver's license and the tow truck will be here any moment to pick up the car. That is enough."

The ticket and getting the car back would cost thousands of dollars. I was driving to school to take a shower because I didn't have a place to live.

I was a poor, starving student. I had to figure out how to eat and where to live. McDonald's hired me without legal status. Eventually so would Carl's Jr. and Subway. I went to classes during the day, and in the evening I took the bus for an hour and a half to get to my job. That semester, my grades were the lowest they had ever been. Instead of studying, I stood for hours waiting for the bus, walking miles home in the dark.

The worst part of college was being away from my family. Every time I would walk through the perfectly manicured lawns and the beautiful, spacious parks by my school, I would wish that my sisters were closer so I could take them to the park. My mother would call me every day to tell me bad news, how she got laid off again or how she did not have money to get my little sisters a bed for Christmas. My two youngest sisters were Americans, and still they were sleeping on the floor, just like the men from La Temple. One day my mother called to tell me that my eighteen-year-old sister Rosi was pregnant and about to move in with her Puerto Rican boyfriend.

Even thought I was couch-surfing and eating scraps, I felt guilty living away from them in such a beautiful place when they were living in poverty. I could not tell them that I was in poverty, too, even though it was not visible. I was so hungry and so sad, I just wanted to sleep so I could escape it all.

ONE FROM MANY (E PLURIBUS UNUM)
2005
SANTA ANA, CALIFORNIA

I WASN'T MAKING IT at college. Fees were going up. I couldn't find enough work to pay my bills. I didn't have a stable place to live, bouncing from couch to couch. I was going to as many free student events that had food as I could, just to have something to eat. My budget for food was $2 per day. Some days all I ate was a McChicken or a dollar burger, whatever was the cheapest option on the fast-food menus.

I had gone to college without loans, trying to do it all on my own. I had decided to pursue a degree in literary journalism because I was spending so much time trying to make ends meet that I didn't have time for the rigorous engineering coursework, but it still seemed impossible. I didn't think I was going to make it to graduation, and even if I did, there was no next step. Once I had a degree, I still couldn't legally work. My plan had been to work until the laws changed, but time had run out and nothing had changed.

Just as I was ready to give up, I walked into a community forum full of hope.

"My dreams are not done," a student told the crowd after revealing he had been denied acceptance at medical schools because of his lack of legal status. His name was Ricardo and he wanted to be a doctor, but there was no medical school that would accept undocumented students. "My education continues. I have enrolled in a master's program in public health instead." He then paused and took out a diploma from UC Los Angeles. "This," he said, "is tangible proof that I am not just selling intangible dreams. I will keep fighting."

Minerva then came up to the podium. She was an undocumented student who had fought for in-state tuition and to stop the deportation of undocumented students. Her parents had been deported, and she had stayed behind to finish her education. "Please, please help us," she cried.

I got up from my seat and walked over to Marco Antonio Firebaugh, the man the community forum was meant to give us an opportunity to talk with. He was a member of the California State Assembly and had authored the bill that had allowed me to go to school without having to pay out-of-state tuition. We shook hands and I thanked him.

That day he gave me something else to thank him for as well. For the first time in my life, I heard stories from people like me: high-achieving students, honors students, who were also undocumented, who just wanted to get an education. Thus far in my life, all my friends had had papers. This was the first time I'd seen people sharing their undocumented dreams in public, unashamed.

I introduced myself to Minerva and Ricardo.

"Can I interview you for my class, Ricardo?" I asked.

"I can only help you if you help us," he replied.

I was eager to get my interview but wondered what he meant by helping them. One thing was clear: these young adults were superstars, while I was a dim, dying star slowly gravitating into a black hole. "When shall we start?" I asked.

"Tomorrow. Santa Ana College. 5 p.m."

And that was how I became part of the movement. We were in step one of our liberation: educating the public about our existence. The group was local to Santa Ana, California, but the main organizing force ranged from San Juan Capistrano to the outskirts of Los Angeles and the Inland Empire, including areas in southern California that were typically ultra wealthy and conservative. We had blogs and Yahoo! groups where we would organize.

"Antonia, what do think about this speech?"

"Antonia, can you help write the press release?"

"Antonia, can you look over the website before it goes live?"

"Antonia, take the microphone."

We called ourselves the Orange County DREAM Team coalition. In addition to Ricardo, Minerva, and me, there were around nine other active members. When we introduced ourselves, we said we were AB-540 students. That was our common denominator. We were the undocumented kids who got in-state tuition, who were trying to share our stories in order to help pass any policy that would help us become contributing members of society.

We became like brothers and sisters. We spent night and day together. When I graduated college that spring, they were the people who came to my ceremony.

Graduating college felt nothing like graduating high school.

29

Without being able to get a job, there was nothing to look forward to. Instead, I put all of my energy into helping the OC Dream Team find a solution for our future.

We had heard about proposed legislation that was introduced in 2001 to give young undocumented people a chance for an education. We dug into the history to discover what happened to it. What we found was a complicated story.

The bill was first introduced by a Democrat in Illinois, Luis Gutiérrez, but went through subsequent versions, each of which gained more Democratic and Republican cosponsors and votes. On August 1, 2001, bill S. 1291 was introduced by U.S. Senators Dick Durbin (D-Illinois) and Orrin Hatch (R-Utah) under a shortened name—the Development, Relief, and Education for Alien Minors Act. The DREAM Act was born. At the same time, Mexican president Vicente Fox was in conversations with George W. Bush about the possibility of amnesty for undocumented immigrants.

Then, in a single day, the whole world changed. On September 11, 2001, two planes piloted by immigrants crashed into the Twin Towers. They were legal immigrants, trained and supported in the American system. At first, Muslims were blamed for the attacks. But soon, all immigrants became targets of the public's anger about what had happened, and discussions about any sort of immigration reform were dropped.

The terrorist attacks of 9/11 had affected us all—even as undocumented Americans, we'd felt it in our hearts. On top of all that our country had lost, we had also lost our chance to live and work legally. But we weren't going to give up.

THE DREAMER
2005-2007
ANAHEIM, LOS ANGELES, SANTA ANA, PASADENA, BAKERSFIELD, AND SAN FRANCISCO, CALIFORNIA

TOGETHER WE CREATED a future for our shared dream. None of us knew anything about politics, but we had a common struggle. We struggled day after day, year after year. We needed to let people know that we were going to organize every day until we helped ourselves and our community. As we shared our stories, we got invited to more and more presentations, giving one or two per day.

On Thanksgiving Day, we were invited to speak to a crowd that came together at the Arrowhead Pond of Anaheim. The event was sponsored by Frank Garcia and the Mighty Ducks of Anaheim and offered a free Thanksgiving dinner to all. Frank told us we had three minutes to talk about being Dreamers in order to gain some visibility so that the people of California knew we existed.

They handed us each a microphone. My heart was beating in my chest—it was my first time ever speaking publicly, and it was in front of 15,000 people. I thought about what I learned in high school about giving speeches, and I looked out over the crowd without looking into anyone's eyes. We raised our voices together, each reciting a sentence of the speech we'd practiced for hours:

"We would like to thank Senators Richard Durbin, Chuck Hagel, and Richard Lugar for the introduction of S. 2075, the DREAM Act of 2005 in the Senate. Support us. We will not let the DREAM Act be forgotten in the Senate again."

People clapped. The message resounded at the speech and in the hearts of those who were hopeful with the reintroduction of the DREAM Act.

The DREAM Act of 2005 did not make it out of the Senate, but it gave us a name. We were now called Dreamers. I was now part of a generation of young undocumented immigrants, the 1.5 generation, who were allowed to dream.

When the Sensenbrenner Bill passed the House that December, we took over the streets. The bill was devastating to the immigrant community and a threat to estimated eleven million of us who would be affected. It would make it a felony to reside in the U.S. without legal status. It would also make it a crime to aid or harbor an undocumented person—people would be told to turn us in, like in Germany when they turned in the Jews.

Millions of us took to the streets to protest during the following months. Some called us the sleeping giant, a conglomeration of mixed-status families and their allies along with the millions of undocumented workers who had quietly existed through the last two decades. It had been twenty years since Reagan's amnesty. Hostility toward immigrants had reached a high point, and we were no longer safe in the shadows.

My family marched in the streets of Chicago. I marched in Los Angeles and in Santa Ana. Together we marched. Together we pleaded:

"No to the Sensenbrenner Bill!"

"What do we want? Legalization! When do we want it? Now!"

"No somos uno, no somos cien. Somos millones. ¡Cuéntenos bien! We aren't one, we aren't one hundred. We are millions. Count us!"

In Santa Ana, I was introduced as a Dreamer and was handed the megaphone. "Tell them about the DREAM Act. Give them hope."

"I am Antonia Rivera," I began. "I am part of the 1.5 generation. I am undocumented. I live in a mixed-status family. I am here because I believe that I can make a difference if I share my story."

The Sensenbrenner Bill was defeated in the Senate in 2006, but there was always more to do. I was working day and night on teams to help immigrant rights. The DREAM Act was what I wanted most, but I also wanted to fight for us all. I was working with a national-level team on comprehensive immigration reform (CIR), a separate but connected team on the DREAM Act, a state-level team to pass a driver's license bill, and another team to pass a financial aid bill for undocumented students in California. I also helped initiate a network of student groups called the CA DREAM Network.

We were willing to do and give anything for the cause. Every single thing in my life revolved around immigrant rights. If I went to dinner, it was for work. If I went to a party, it was an event or a fundraiser. One hour I would be on a call with Washington, DC, organizations; the next I would be at meetings with local organizers in LA. I took calls into the night. We presented to national groups of educators, mental health professionals, and more.

Time was finite. The team needed to gain national attention.

32

A lot of people still did not know about our situations or about the DREAM Act. We were aging, our parents were aging, and we had no place to go.

Even as we were all Dreamers, our situations were diverse. We had more layers than the slogans and sound bites were able to give. For example, my friend Hermina came to the United States in the 1990s to join her father, who had amnesty already, and he applied for amnesty for her when she was twelve. Each year a limited number of parental petition visas are granted, and when the visas are gone, the people left on the list are bumped to the next year. If you never receive the visa while you are a child, you move into the adult category once you turn eighteen. The adult category has a smaller number of visas and a longer wait. Hermina had aged out of her child–parent amnesty petition. Over six years she'd waited, and now she was on the adult list. The DREAM Act would help her and others like her.

So many of us had these stories. But for us, they were not just stories. They were our lives.

We wanted DREAM, and we also wanted comprehensive immigration reform because it would include the rest of our families. We were willing to put our bodies on the line. We decided we were going to fast in order to get cosponsors for the DREAM Act and for comprehensive reform.

"Welcome to the Students Fast for Immigration Reform launch stop. We will not eat food for a week in solidarity." We were going to fast outside the San Francisco City Hall and talk to as many politicians as we could. One team would work as a traveling caravan and another would stay in San Francisco. I was the organizer for the first stop in Santa Ana.

"We have attempted to set up a meeting with the legislators or their staff along this path, but many have refused. So let's go!" I said with a firm voice.

We were armed with banners. Armed with our voices.

"¿Qué queremos? El DREAM Act. ¿Cuándo? Ahora. What do we want? DREAM Act! When do we want it? Now."

"Education. No deportation!"

"¡Somos estudiantes! ¡Peleando por justicia! ¡Respeto y dignidad! We are students! Fighting for justice and our education! What do we want? Justice! Justice! Now!"

Dianne Feinstein was one of the California senators, and Loretta Sanchez was my district's representative. We would start by visiting Loretta, and then we would go to Feinstein.

Carload after carload arrived at the calm office nestled amid white fences.

"Loretta! Loretta! Come on out! See what the DREAM Act is all about!" we yelled from outside, hopeful.

The windows of her office went from light to dark. They closed the blinds.

We were notified by her chief of staff that he would talk with the two paid organizers and two DREAM beneficiaries. The group decided I was one of the Dreamers they wanted to send.

I told him about our plight, that we desperately needed someone to cosponsor the DREAM Act. His impatience was clear as he said, "Loretta is running for reelection. She supports DREAM, but part of her district is conservative and she has a tough reelection coming up."

This was always the problem. Our representatives would tell us they supported something on a private vote but were unwilling to cosponsor a bill because votes mattered more.

We pressed him again about cosponsoring, and suddenly he changed. His face twisted as he accused us of being selfish. "What about your parents? Loretta is working behind closed doors on a comprehensive immigration reform bill. It is different from the ones that have been presented. We told you already. Why would you want to push for DREAM when we are already working on something to help not only you but everyone?"

"Where is the bill?" we shouted. "When is it coming out? Show the bill!"

"You are selfish! I am done," the chief of staff said as he stormed out. It hurt to be called selfish—we were fighting for everyone. But we needed DREAM now. We couldn't work or be part of society without it. We also didn't believe that the bills they were promising us would ever really come.

Unfortunately, it was the same story with Dianne Feinstein and her office.

We fasted for six days in an attempt to get cosponsors for CIR and DREAM. There were many of us. Mario was a UCLA student who had lived through the Central American war. Ernesto was fasting for his younger brothers without status. Rodrigo in his Che Guevara hat was lighting candles for the vigil. Many of them had come as children like me.

We ended our ceremony with a mock graduation in front of the San Francisco City Hall. Our last words were, "I will stop organizing for the DREAM Act and start organizing for something that is going to help a larger immigrant community."

On the sixth day, I had broth.

THE REBEL

2007-2010

WASHINGTON, DC; ORANGE COUNTY, ANAHEIM, AND SANTA ANA, CALIFORNIA

I WALKED into the Center for Community Change meeting, holding my breath. "Should I tell the youth what just happened?" I asked myself aloud.

I was in DC to fight for my life and that of my community. But nothing in politics was simple, and I was growing disillusioned. By chance, I had just been part of a call between Dick Durbin and representatives from think tanks. He said something like, "I need you to mobilize your base. I am thinking about reintroducing the DREAM Act. Can you help me gather cosponsors?"

The leads on the call replied with something like, "We have decided that the best way to pass DREAM is as an attachment, not as a stand-alone bill."

"But we have a delegation of about thirteen potential DREAM Act beneficiaries on their way to DC. Why can't we wait to ask them for their input?" the organizer that I was with asked.

35

"No," the think tanks insisted.

"Then what is the purpose of us being here, if we are not going to be invited to the bargaining table?" I wondered.

I had thought that we would be fighting the Republicans, but the people who were supposed to be on our side weren't fighting for us. The people who were speaking on behalf of my community weren't helping us. They were helping themselves.

My mother used to always tell me that politicians were corrupt in Mexico, but in the United States, they were much cleaner. But I was realizing it wasn't that simple, that politicians here had agendas and reelection to worry about. Politics here wasn't just about doing what was right; it was about winning.

I kept quiet about the call as I welcomed people to the meeting. My plane ticket had been paid for. I was here as labor. I was going to help them even if they would not help me because I was not going to turn down an opportunity that could help the immigrant community.

But when I went back to California, I was heartbroken. I wanted to give up.

At the state level my opinion had mattered, but at the national level, there were other people who had the last word about what I needed, what my family needed. The California DREAM Act was not passed. I had worked to help get Obama elected, but now it looked like change would not be coming from his administration, either. I felt old and tired from the fight.

"Antonia, we are warriors. You can't give up. I have set up an appointment with a mental health professional," Ricardo said. He was no longer involved in the movement, but he had heard that I was not doing well.

After therapy, I decided to break off from the politicians and the organizers. I didn't want to be part of anyone else's narrative. I wanted to tell my own story.

I wanted to put together my own DREAM team, the team of my dreams. I needed more warriors like the warrior I had become. People who were not just cherry-picked to be poster children. People who chose to be warriors on their own because they believed in the fight. Warriors like the ones on the Orange County DREAM Team, people who would sit at the bargaining table in a circle, not a hierarchical power structure.

I sent invitations to people I knew might need a place to belong: "We would like to invite you to a meeting to possibly renew the collaborative efforts between LA and OC to continue supporting the rights of undocumented students. We believe that you are important to the cause."

The first meeting was packed. There were new warriors and warriors who came out of retirement. There were best friends and allies. Many of them had been part of the LA DREAM team that was no longer in existence.

We formed DREAM Team LA to collaborate with the Orange County DREAM Team. Together, both DREAM teams helped launch a national youth-led movement called The Dream Is Coming. We would collaborate with an online group called Dream Activist, and for the first time ever, we would use social media for the movement. We were ready to lead the rest of the Dreamers around the country.

I was ready for the fight of my life.

I used my savings to book tickets for myself and two others to Washington, DC, where we would attend the United We Dream graduation ceremony—a mock graduation of Dreamers to raise awareness of our struggle. But our real goal was to get meetings with the most powerful people in Congress. We wanted them to help us push forward the DREAM.

I slept on the cold floor of a church. I thought back to everything that I had lived through. My Facebook update that day kept repeating in my head: *I am still "nine digits away from my dream."* . . . *It has been a bittersweet journey and I have given a lot up for DREAM, including [being with] my family in the Midwest. But I feel the DREAM is coming not just for me but also for my younger sister and friends* . . .

The next day we requested a face-to-face meeting with Dianne Feinstein. Her staff said we could not meet with her, so we decided to hold a sit-in at her office. Nineteen Dreamers dressed in graduation gowns formed a circle around two bold signs that read, "DREAM ACT now. UNDOCUMENTED AND UNAFRAID."

Our message wasn't directed to the Republicans but to the nonprofits and the Democrats, who weren't allowing us to lobby for the DREAM Act as a stand-alone bill.

First came a reporter. Then a social worker. Then the Capitol Police. I heard their command to shut the entrances to the building. Staffers and lobbyists from all seven floors ran out of their offices to see what was going on. I looked up and saw them staring down at me from the rows and rows of balconies overlooking the atrium where I quietly sat with twenty other undocumented people.

The flashes of phones became overwhelming. My eyes slid to the dark sculpture behind me, to the blue uniforms that were beginning to appear in front and to the sides of me. I shut my eyes as I heard the final command from the police: "IF YOU DO NOT MOVE, WE WILL ARREST YOU."

I heard the sniffs of a girl who walked away to avoid detention—I knew she was not a coward, but she had to protect herself more than the rest of us. She stood by on the sidelines. I sank deeper into the floor and closed my eyes. When I opened them, I saw a flurry of black, gold, and blue graduation gowns. I saw wrists being put in plastic handcuffs. A voice told me stand up. I felt the snap on my wrist.

As the police took me to a white van, the social worker yelled from the other side of the building, "Antonia! Be strong!" Students who had traveled for the graduation stood on the sidelines and chanted, "Undocumented! Unafraid!"

They took us to the back of a building that looked like a warehouse. We were each assigned our own police escort.

"Who told you to do this? Who are you working for?" One by one, we were taken to a table and asked these questions.

"We aren't working for anyone," we said. They could not believe we would put our bodies in that type of danger on our own. But I was there because I wanted to be. I was there because I thought I had nothing to lose.

They began to take down our information on pads of paper.

38

One of the officers explained that it would be a misdemeanor and that we would be ticketed and released, but then he asked for two forms of ID.

I had my Mexican passport but nothing else. Another boy had the same.

"This is going to be an actual arrest for you now. I am sorry," the officer said to us. "The rest of you can go," he said to the younger protestors who had produced student IDs.

Real handcuffs were snapped on my wrists, and I was put in the back of a police car. At the jail, I was put in front of a kiosk with a laser that scanned my eyes and my body. They attached my handcuffs to a bar.

It was chaos. I heard them speaking about a massive arrest and about how we were undocumented. I heard them say it was the first time undocumented immigrants were arrested for protesting. There was no protocol. They didn't know what forms to fill out.

I closed my eyes. ICE could be called any minute and I could be deported, sent to a place where I had nothing. I might never see my family again. I began to cry. Our stories were not campaigns. They weren't talking points. We needed DREAM and CIR to survive. But now it had come to the point where I'd put my life in danger. Tears streamed down my face. What had I done?

THE WOUNDED WARRIOR
2010-2011
SANTA ANA, CALIFORNIA

I WAS NOT DEPORTED. I got out of jail and fell into the arms of those waiting outside for me. Crowds outside the jail cheered at our release. I just wanted to go home.

The news reports were coming in like hail. I flew back to California to hold press conferences and conduct interviews. The news reached me that Durbin and other politicians were disappointed because we had not talked to them before putting ourselves in danger. I could not believe what I was hearing. We had asked everyone for help—politicians, nonprofits, the unions, everyone. We had even attended the Reform Immigration for America (RIFA) fundraiser with LA mayor Antonio Villaraigosa, the National Council of La Raza, and movie directors, asking for help, but when they took no action, we finally we had to do something on our own.

In the weeks that followed, the news of our arrest incited a national media frenzy. The LA and OC DREAM Team activities only increased momentum, holding hunger strikes outside congressional offices. There were actions occurring across the country as the fight for DREAM reached a fever pitch.

At the same time, I began to collapse. I became sick and felt more tired than I had been in a long time. I felt empty inside. For the first time in my life, I was afraid, really afraid. During everything I had been through, even when I was little, I always felt in control. For the first time, a force larger than me had taken me in its hold. I felt I should be at the heart of the fight, but I just wanted to hide.

Home, however, was suddenly not a place I could hide. I had been dating a man from Michoacán—an immigrant too, but he had assimilated down. Instead of improving his life here, his time in the U.S. had hurt him emotionally, and he'd gotten involved with the wrong people. He was angry and struggling. I thought I could help him, but his mental health was proving more than I could handle, and my arrest sent him into a place of aggression and control. Angry that I joined the demonstration, he started to hurt me. At first, it was a push. Then a slap. And then a jab with a knife and a loaded gun pointed at my head.

I tried leaving, but he would always come looking for me. I knew he was mentally ill and that he needed help, but I had nothing left to give. I wanted to stay even further away from the movement because I was afraid he would come to the meetings and everyone would see, or worse, that he would hurt the cause and it would be my fault. I stayed away, trying to deal with all the things inside me and in my personal life.

When the nonprofits, unions, and politicians finally announced they would help us pass the DREAM Act as a stand-alone bill,

I was not there. They announced that they would still work on comprehensive reform, but they would try to pass our bill on its own. After ten years of fighting, when they finally "freed the DREAM," I did not celebrate, did not hug my teammates, did not cry or laugh or raise a glass in celebration with my team. I was in one of the darkest moments of my life.

My mother and my sisters came to visit me in California. My baby sisters were now teenagers, and Rosi had her own little family. At the same time, I also celebrated my ten-year high school reunion. I asked about the valedictorian from the class of 2000, the boy I'd spoken with on the bus who'd confessed his status to me, but no one knew where he had gone. I imagined he had been deported. The rest of the honors kids were now working professionals. They said that I was the Martin Luther King of the class. I smiled, but I was ashamed. I was in a violent relationship and did not know how to ask for help. It felt like everyone looked up to me. Make-up. I needed make-up.

While my friends continued with the movement, I began to work an 8-to-5 job making phone calls for the DREAM Act. It was a way to keep helping while staying away from the front line. Progress seemed to be coming, but it was slow—the DREAM Act passed the House but failed to gain enough votes in the Senate. I did one last interview. "Hello, my name is Antonia . . ."

When the bill was presented in the Senate, I realized it was different. As I read through the bill, I saw they had added more requirements, including an age cap of thirty. I could not believe my eyes. I let the hurdle I was facing sink in—I was twenty-eight years old. Even if the bill I'd spent all these years fighting for did finally pass in the next few years, I could be aged out of qualifying. By the time it became law, chances were high that I would be thirty, which meant that even if larger reform passed, I would have to wait two or three times longer to become a legal permanent resident than someone who qualified under the DREAM Act.

My deep sadness and emptiness somehow found a way further down. I could not wait that long to work and begin my life. There was a sad irony in all of this—they'd always called us Dreamers "kids," because those were the stories that resonated, but they'd waited so long that many of us were adults, and now we might not even be saved by what we had been fighting for.

I lost another job. The recession was in full force. Work was scarce and companies were going out of business overnight. I stood in line for seven hours to get a hostess job at a restaurant that would hire undocumented people. I got it, once again working in the food service industry. Everyone working there had a degree.

At the same time, the Obama administration was increasing deportations for everyone, not just people with criminal records. Without any status or protection, I was still at risk of deportation. I felt the pressure closing in on me from all sides: the arrest, my relationship, the age cap added to the bill, the threat of deportation at any moment. The fight for the DREAM Act was becoming a fight just to stop deportations. The raids had become so common. One part of the government said they were fighting to help us and DREAM, while another part was arresting us and sending us away. More and more of my friends, even those with college degrees, were getting ankle bracelets and put on removal proceedings.

From the sidelines, I tried to help my team look for alternatives to bills. We had always been told that only Congress could create laws to give us freedom, but one of our team members had begun to work with lawyers to see if we could be liberated through an executive order. If we could find an alternative to the long congressional process, we could save ourselves and maybe be able to help our parents, too. Still, no matter how much I tried, I could not find the energy to keep fighting. It seemed that at every corner there was a new roadblock and that the fight would never end.

I fell into a deep depression. I wanted to disappear, but I was still known in the movement, and people wanted my help. I would get calls to make appearances, that I was needed for one more thing, to do one more interview, be in one more meeting, on one more call. It was hard to say no and even harder to put on a smile I didn't feel inside. I helped because I wanted relief for all of us, but I felt as empty inside as I ever had.

Finally the Obama administration issued a memorandum saying they would not seek to deport people with no criminal records. It was a tiny victory. I watched as the news came through the community. I looked around and saw new warriors who had come into the movement, new faces with new energy. It finally felt like we had empowered enough undocumented leaders and allies to be unashamed and unafraid. There were people taking my place, and I was ready to let them take the reins. I was ready to focus on my own healing and to find peace. I couldn't lead a movement, I couldn't help my boyfriend, and I couldn't help other immigrants until I helped myself. And if was going help myself, I had to step out of this world completely. I needed to be anonymous. But where could I go?

Some years before, my uncle had been looking to leave the craze of Chicago for someplace calmer. He was always the visionary in the family, the one who saw into the future and who scouted new places and led our family to them. He was the first to say that maybe cities weren't right for us anymore. He had read a newspaper article about how Iowa was forecasted to be one of the best places to live in by 2010. I was only nineteen then, and Iowa with its tiny towns built around *matanzas* wasn't a big draw for me, but I set out with him on a scouting trip.

It hadn't been love at first sight with Iowa. I was a suburban teen, and to me, Iowa looked like a dying old man with no heirs and Des Moines like an old Victorian lady desperately trying to recuperate the charm of her once-splendid homes with paint-stripped shutters. I did not see the prospective revival that the article mentioned, but we were there and ready to find out what was possible from the other locals. We waited outside a Catholic church that had a Spanish mass sign to see if we could find anyone who could help us find work and apartments. When mass was over, people flooded out into the parking lot and my uncle asked them, "*¿Oye, en qué trabajan por aquí? ¿Y adónde viven?* Hey, what do you guys do for work around here? Where do you live?"

They told us which McDonald's and which factories were hiring Latinos. After that, we went to look at places to live. In a single weekend trip we'd found jobs and apartments, and my uncle decided to move his family.

Now here I was, a decade later. I wanted to be anonymous. I wanted to be able to walk outside without anyone knowing who I was. I needed a place to heal, to take some time for myself. A place where I could work on my own personal healing. My boyfriend had control over me, the movement had control over me, the politicians had control over me, the nonprofits had control over me. I thought to myself, maybe this is what my mother felt back in Mexico. I was ready to start a new life and be free of it all.

I said goodbye one last time to my beloved California with its palm trees, salty waters, and cool Santa Ana winds. Beloved California, with streets bearing Spanish surnames, lined with beautiful white missions. Beloved California, with its golden homes concealing the maids and gardeners, their sweat and tears. Beloved. Beloved. Beloved. As I said goodbye, I imagined that this was how first-generation immigrants like my mother must have felt when they left their home country to begin again in a new place, unsure of what it had to offer but with great hope for survival. It was time to start a new life.

THE IOWAN
2011-2012
DES MOINES, IOWA

HOME WAS FIRST in the North of Mexico City. Then it was in the West of the United States. Now it would be in the Midwest. I took the *Grapes of Wrath* path but in reverse order. Everything seemed out of place. As I looked at the city of Des Moines through the airplane window, I felt my lungs breathing within my heart, sad for what I was leaving behind.

Iowa offered something new. In California and Chicago, we always had to live stacked on top of each other, renting rooms in our apartments to friends or even some random person who answered our ads just so we could afford to live there. Here we could have our own place.

My mom was looking for a job. The recession had hit Illinois and she couldn't find work, so she came to Iowa. My sister Rosi was a young mom having a hard time with her boyfriend in Chicago, and she wanted to go somewhere quieter than that scene. So we

44

were all here now.

Within a few months after my move, I got a job, bought a couch, and moved into my own studio apartment on the south side of Des Moines. It was 500 square feet of 1950s charm, a place with huge windows and natural light, a place to call home for my puppy and myself.

At first, Iowa felt like I was going back in time. It felt like California in the 1980s and 1990s, when I lived in Anaheim as a kid. There were no big Mexican stores, and the regular stores didn't sell anything Mexican. I wasn't sure I would know how to live in a place so different from where I had been, but before I knew it, I began to fall in love with the possibilities.

To my surprise, Iowa, the state that had seemed like an old man when I visited ten years earlier, had been reborn, and Des Moines was undergoing a cultural revival. The newspaper article that had prompted my uncle to come here was right, Iowa was indeed becoming a place people wanted to move to. Like me, people had heard that it was where you could raise a family and have a better quality of life than in the big cities. Masses of young professionals were scrambling back to the Midwest to escape the housing market crash that had plagued the metropolitan areas, bringing with them new ideas of the things they did not want to live without. Over the dirt roads I had once seen were sidewalks and parks. From the dark, abandoned buildings downtown, there grew lofts with a chic New York feel. In a way I had never imagined, it began to feel like a place I could call home.

In March, I went back to California to visit. My boyfriend was getting out of jail and claimed he had been rehabilitated, but seeing him made me realize that he was not yet okay. I wanted to break up, but I still did not know how. I told him we could continue a long-distance relationship, but I had a life in Iowa now.

Later that spring, I discovered that my visit to California would change my life forever: I was pregnant.

I invited my mother and sisters over to my apartment and gave them the news. I was going to be an undocumented mother. It was nerve-racking, but I was thirty years old and could not pass up what seemed like my last chance to become a mother. I was determined to live a normal life, with or without papers. Deportation, however, remained close in my mind. President Obama was in the middle of his reelection campaign, and around the country, my friends were participating in sit-ins at his campaign office.

On June 15, 2012, I tuned into breaking national news: from the Rose Garden of the White House, President Obama announced a policy that would allow certain immigrants to escape deportation and obtain work permits for a period of two years, renewable upon good behavior. To apply, we had to be younger than thirty-one, must have come to the U.S. when we were younger than sixteen, and must have lived in the U.S. since 2007. I would qualify, along with an estimated 1.7 million others.

The policy, later known as DACA (Deferred Action for Childhood Arrivals), was not a long-term answer, but it would protect me, and now my soon-to-be baby, in the short term. It would give me a work permit. It would allow me to get a driver's license. For the first time in my life, I would have a protected legal presence in the United States.

I watched the online live stream of the DREAM Team press conference and saw one of my friends holding a sign that said, "Obama, don't deport my mama." I felt my belly wiggle.

THE MOTHER
2012
DES MOINES, IOWA

AT THIRTY-ONE WEEKS PREGNANT, I went to a check-up a few days after getting a ticket for driving without a license. I had filled out my application for DACA, but until it was processed, I still was driving without a license. I had just put down a deposit on an apartment, and I was worried about coming up with an extra $300 dollars that month to pay for the ticket.

My midwife came in, saying, "Lie down again." But it was no use. My blood pressure was incredibly high, and they could not figure out why.

"Drive straight to the hospital," she said. "I am transferring your file to the doctors at Iowa Methodist."

At the hospital, they checked me into a room. They told me I had preeclampsia—my kidney enzymes and blood pressure were too high, putting me and the baby at risk.

The first doctors said I would have to have a C-section. I was terrified. I had never had surgery for anything, and I still didn't know how I was going to pay for the birth. I'd applied for assistance from the hospital, but this was months before my due date and nothing had been approved.

Finally, another doctor came in. "You can still have a natural birth," she said. "I talked to the other doctors, and we'll induce the day after tomorrow."

On schedule, I was induced. Everything happened fast—she was coming.

"Did you get an epidural?" the doctor asked. "No? That's okay, there's no time, you are having this baby without it."

My mother, my brother-in-law, and my younger sisters left the room, leaving only my sister Rosi to hold my hand. I pushed and in a moment I released my child into the hands of twenty doctors and nurses, who methodically hooked her up to an artificial environment and rolled her away. The magnesium sulfate I'd taken for my high blood pressure took hold, and my eyes closed.

"Antonia, wake up, we are going to take you to see your baby," a nurse said.

As we rolled up the NICU, another nurse cooed to my tiny girl, "Sweet baby, why are you trying to take off your tubes again? You need this to breathe."

I looked at my little girl inside a clear plastic box. She was so small, only three pounds. The nurse continued, "Can I have your foot? We will be hooking you up to an IV so we don't have to poke you every few hours. Is that okay?"

I watched as my tiny human continued fighting the tube that hooked her up to an oxygen tank. "She is a sassy one," the nurse told me with a giggle. "She may be tiny, but she loves to fight me. Don't feel odd about me talking to her and not you. She's my patient. Even though she is small, she is listening. Would you like to say something to her?"

My head was spinning and my body was limp, the magnesium sulfate in my blood making me drowsy. "Did I actually birth her? Am I a mother?" I asked.

"Of course you are. No medicine can provide the same nutrients that she needs from your body. Now go rest," the nurse said.

I gazed at my creation. I could not hold her, hug her, or kiss her, but she was mine. I would name her Ciel, which means sky in Spanish. Like the sky, she held the moon and the stars up, open with possibilities.

They told me she would stay for at least two months. I drove myself home from the hospital and arrived alone at my bare apartment. I looked at the lone piece of furniture, my couch. I had no paid maternity leave. No PTO. I was an undocumented mother who had birthed a tiny warrior. My body no longer belonged to any movement or anyone but her.

After DACA passed, I had started a group for young DACA recipients and their friends and family. I'd organized it within the American Friends Service Committee, a Quaker group focused on social issues. Originally I started it to provide support to others, but while I was waiting for my baby to come home, when I needed a work permit more than ever, I was told my DACA application was held up because of my arrest in Washington, DC.

The day Ciel came home from the hospital, I went to work at the front desk of a hotel. While I waited for the decision on my DACA status, I had no choice but to continue with undocumented work. With a minimum-wage job, I had a baby with medical needs, my apartment and car, and everything else in our lives to pay. The days were a blur, alternating first, second, and third shifts. Sometimes I slept during the day, sometimes at night, waking only to feed Ciel or to pump for her. My body and mind were in a daze, pumping without a lunch break, breast milk oozing through my blue-collared blouse at the front desk, with no one to relieve me from my post. At home, the winter cold came, and I realized that our apartment, the only one that did not ask us for a background check, was not insulated, and I was too afraid to sleep because the ceiling was caving in over my little girl's bed.

THE DACA-MENTED EMPLOYEE
2018
DES MOINES, IOWA

I WAS DACAmented, for the moment. My status was approved when Ciel was eight months old. I owned a home with furniture. I had a child who attended preschool at the Science Center, who woke up every day and looked forward to life in Iowa: strolling at the Blank Park Zoo, dancing to Parranderos Latin Combo during Jazz in July, eating pizza at Cici's or clam chowder at Waterfront Seafood market. But I was still in survivor mode. I lived in constant fear. The weekend I received my approval from DACA, I also got word that Ciel's father had been deported. From that point on, her relationship with her birth father would be limited to video conference.

With my work permit, I was able to get an entry-level position as an analyst at Well Fargo. It was nothing close to the engineering career that I'd once hoped for, but it was a steady job with benefits that allowed me to provide for my family.

After the election in 2016, there was real fear in our immigrant community. The atmosphere toward immigrants felt like the days after 9/11 all over again. My life felt like a vicious cycle, reminding me of when I was eight years old on the couch in La Temple and being called a criminal, only now I was watching a soon-to-be president calling me a criminal, a drug dealer, and a rapist. I looked over at my baby daughter and promised to spend my life showing her that those words were not true.

On June 16, 2017, the Trump administration announced they intended to review the DACA policy, and two months later they announced it would be repealed. The language they used was "phased out." What that meant in real terms was that once our DACA status was gone, ICE could take us away from the country we'd grown up in, the home where our lives and families were. Did the American people understand what was happening?

That same fall, Wells Fargo held a company conference on diversity and inclusion. Up to that point, I had worked quietly in the background, just doing my job each day and trying to stay in my corner. No one I worked with knew my story or realized what that announcement had meant for me and my family. I walked through the crowds at the conference, recognizing many familiar faces from the last five years of my employment, yet feeling alone, never having made a close friend at work.

The conference got underway in a giant ballroom full of people, and finally it came time for audience questions for the panelists. My heart trembled and my whole body shook. I heard my blood rush to my ears. I did not know if I would be able to talk into that microphone and introduce myself as effortlessly as I had in the past whenever I had felt a need to say something.

"We have time for one more question," I heard them say. I stood up.

"I am Antonia, and I am partly undocumented. I have lived in this country without legal status for thirty years. Today I have a work permit but no legal status." My voice resonated loudly over the silence of 1,200 corporate employees as I explained that my status was tenuous and asked how to make up for the time I'd lost in the workforce by just trying to survive.

When I was finished, there was silence. Then the panelists answered my question as best as they could. As I took my seat again, I felt my shaking subside. I didn't have a solution, but I was visible again. I had shared my truth. I knew that if people were to understand my status and how to work with DACAmented employees, for them to understand how we lived in limbo, we had to share our stories.

THE SURVIVOR
2019
DES MOINES, IA

I AM THIRTY-SEVEN YEARS OLD. I live with my daughter in our house, yellow with piercing orange trim, prairie tulips and sweet honey wheat growing in our yard.

My life in Iowa revolves around my family and my work. From

the outside, it is a normal life. On the inside, I live in survival mode, in constant limbo waiting for a status that protects me for more than two years at a time, waiting for the latest policy decision, waiting for a change that may never come.

We never passed the DREAM Act. It is hard for people like me to not get hurt within the political system—our voices get drowned out by the voices in power. Marginalized people, people like me who need help to be seen by the government, need politicians and allies who listen and then let us speak for ourselves instead of using our stories and our lives as bargaining chips. We need Americans to hear from us personally, to understand our stories and their complexity directly from us.

DACA saved some of us, but only in the short term. It was clean and didn't have any of the complications of congressional bills, but it also only applied to a small group of the immigration population who needed status. In my case, even though it wasn't the dream we crusaded for, it provided temporary relief. It gave me a work permit, a driver's license, and a sense of dignity that I was part of the system and contributing to society, something that I'd wanted for as long as I could remember. Today I have a job and PTO. When my grandmother died, I was able to mourn. I have paid holidays and can actually be at home on Christmas with my family. I have benefits—I can take my daughter to the doctor, and I have health care for myself.

But I live every day knowing my life here could come to an end. DACA is temporary protection—the current administration has stated it will repeal the policy, and no new applications are being taken. The repeal is currently on hold with lawsuits from states on both sides of the issue. In the meantime, ICE raids and deportations continue to increase, targeting not just undocumented criminals but in some cases legal residents and even naturalized citizens. We live day by day. We try to go on.

My family and I have started going to therapy to talk about how immigration has affected us as a family. My mom is undocumented, I have DACA status, my younger sister is a legal permanent resident, and my youngest sisters are both U.S. citizens. Living in a mixed-status family affects us all. At any minute, all of this could be taken away. We could be broken apart.

I know people in Iowa, but I don't have a lot of friends here. I try not to have too many friendships because if something ever happens to me, I don't want people to be hurt.

As I grow older, I become less and less the kind of person that the policies and laws will save, just like DACA didn't save my older friends, the original people fighting for DREAM and AB 540. Some of them got married or their parents were finally able to legalize them, while others are still hiding in undocumented jobs, waiting for their time but knowing it may never come. While politicians fight and nonprofits and unions lobby, the problems go on. We are still here.

My mother, who never got her papers, goes to work even as an old lady. Others will retire, but she never will. She's given her labor to this country for thirty years, and she will work until she can't anymore. There is such little hope for me, but even less for her. As Latinos we don't send our parents to retirement homes—we are their retirement. As long as I am here, I will take care of her.

Iowa has been my safe haven. I have found refuge here like so many others. Just the other day, I ran into a little Mexican boy who said, "I love it here. It's so quiet. It's so lovely." I smiled and told him I agreed. At the national level, it seems like Iowa isn't included in the immigration talks, except for during the presidential elections—the Latinos here aren't included in the national conversation. But we are here, so many of us, quietly living our lives, owning our own homes and even our own businesses, helping to revitalize dying towns. We're here working the meat-packing plants, working the fields, working construction, and working in places like Wells Fargo, too. We're here doing the work, just like the men of La Temple. As long as American employers want hard workers who won't complain, and American buyers want cheaper products and services, the immigration tug-of-war will never end.

The topic of immigration has no simple solution because lives of people aren't simple things to just vote in or out. When the U.S. created the Bracero Program, inviting Mexicans to come here to work, they didn't consider the long-term effects. They didn't plan for American employers to continue recruiting *braceros*. They also didn't plan for cultural considerations. For many Mexicans, the family unit has been recentered in the United States. Our grandmothers have died; the people we wanted to go back to visit are gone. Culturally we are expected to stay together. We follow our families. We survive together.

Today, politicians are still trying to create new versions of the Bracero Program to bring seasonal workers here to fill American labor needs. The truth that no one wants to talk about is that without the immigrant labor force, the country could not run. Yet with workers will come families, because you cannot bring people in to do your hard labor without side effects. The cycle never ends.

For so many of us, the United States is the only home we know. For me, the safety of this country is why I love it most. I want to give to this country, to invest my time and talents here. I want to be free. I want to travel to Mexico without needing advance parole and to know the place I was born without fear, but at the end of the day, the U.S. is where I belong. This is where my life is. It's where I played the clarinet in the high school band, where I ran cross country, where I walked across the stage to get my degree. It's where I had my first kiss, my first job, my first house. It's where my daughter breathed her first breath.

I was part of a movement, a fight for the rights and lives of immigrants in this country. I joined the movement because I was here without status, because I crossed the border as a child. I was a little girl with a free heart who followed her family because she didn't know any better. Back then, children like me were a rarity—my sister and I were the only ones we knew our age who crossed.

Today, that is not the case. Our laws were not written for what we are experiencing now. They were not written to deal with the humanitarian crisis of the southern countries and the wave of children coming daily to our border. Right now, at our border, we have children in camps like prisons. Even if they are three years old, they will go in front of a judge, and the judge will rule on them in the same way they would an adult.

Whatever each of us believes about immigration, we know in our hearts that children should be treated as children, and that after camps, chain-link cells, ICE, and trials, many of these children will never be the same. Things are happening in those camps that should never happen to anyone, much less children. History will remember what we do in this moment and how we protect those who need it most.

There are childhood arrivals at every age level who need special arrival laws; they need protection. For the children who have already crossed the border, for those who have lived part or all of their lives here, they need more than temporary protection that can be taken away in a moment by a new administration—they need a future. It is estimated that 98,000 kids will graduate from high school this year without legal status, and nearly 800,000 people are in limbo awaiting the fate of DACA.

Every day children cross the border and put their lives in our hands. I, Antonia, am one of them.

THE LIFE OF AN UNDOCUMENTED IMMIGRANT: A TIMELINE

ANTONIA RIVERA

1982 I am born. In the U.S., *Plyler vs. Doe* rules that undocumented children can attend K-12 schools.

1985 *Leticia A. vs. Board of Regents* rules that the California education system, including universities, must allow undocumented aliens to prove state residency and pay in-state tuition, giving the children of undocumented aliens the right to an education. This will soon be replicated in other states. It also allows undocumented students to apply for Cal Grants, a form of financial aid.

1986 On November 6, the Immigration Reform and Control Act of 1986 (IRCA), or Reagan amnesty, requires employers to attest to their employees' immigration status, makes it illegal to hire or recruit illegal immigrants knowingly, legalizes certain seasonal agricultural undocumented immigrants, and legalizes undocumented immigrants who entered the United States before January 1, 1982. The Immigration and Naturalization Service (INS) estimates that about four million illegal immigrants will apply for legal status through the act and that roughly half of them will be eligible. I grow up with kids whose parents are legalized through the amnesty. They and their parents travel back and forth between the homeland and the U.S to visit grandparents and family. The first-generation immigrants are able to work legally and provide for their kids. Many buy homes, and the number of immigrant-owned businesses booms.

1988 At six years old, I cross the border into the U.S., undocumented.

1990 The *Bradford* decision rules that higher institutions in California can charge undocumented students out-of-state tuition.

On November 29, as an eight-year-old, I watch as the Immigration Act of 1990 is signed into law by George H. W. Bush, increasing overall immigration. It provides family-based immigration visas, employment-based visas, and a diversity visa for immigrants from low-admittance countries; lifts requirements that allow elderly immigrants to take citizenship tests in languages other than English; creates Temporary Protected Status (TPS) for immigrants fleeing extraordinary conditions; and allows people with nonheterosexual orientations to apply for legal permanent status.

1996 The Illegal Immigration Reform and Immigrant Responsibility Act (IIRIRA) allows higher institutions to charge undocumented students in-state tuition. It also establishes a three-year ban for living 180 days to one year in the U.S. without legal presence and a ten-year ban for those residing for more than a year without legal presence, setting the foundation for the deportation system that is in place today.

1999 I move to the Midwest (Stone Park, IL) around Thanksgiving.

2000 In January, I start school in Illinois at Proviso West High School.

In February, I move back to California.

In June, I graduate from Anaheim High School and return to Stone Park.

In August, I visit Iowa for the first time on a scouting trip with my uncle.

2001 On August 1, bill S. 1291, the Development, Relief, and Education for Alien Minors Act, is introduced by U.S. Senators Dick Durbin (D-Illinois) and Orrin Hatch (R-Utah). The DREAM Act is born.

On September 11, I watch on live TV as the second of two planes crashes into the Twin Towers in New York City, another into the Pentagon, and another into a field in Pennsylvania. President George W. Bush and Congress divert from immigration talks with Mexico to instead focus on the war on terrorism, and the DREAM Act loses support while anti-immigrant sentiment overwhelms the country.

On October 12, AB 540 is signed into law in California, allowing undocumented students and U.S. citizens who meet certain requirements to pay in-state tuition at California public colleges and universities.

2002   I start college at UC Irvine in the fall.

2005   On September 28, I attend the OC DREAM Team town hall with state representative Marco Antonio Firebaugh, author of AB 540.

On Thanksgiving Day, I give a short speech at Arrowhead Pond of Anaheim. It is my first time speaking in front of a large crowd (15,000 people).

On December 16, the Sensenbrenner Bill (H.R. 4437) passes the House of Representatives. It would make it a felony to reside in the U.S. without legal status. It would also make it a crime to aid or harbor an undocumented person.

2006   Over a period of eight weeks, millions of people nationwide participate in what are known as immigration protest Great Marches over the Sensenbrenner Bill. On March 10, my mom and sisters attend the Great March in Chicago. On April 25, I attend the Great March in Los Angeles. On May 1, I help organize the May 1st March in Santa Ana.

On June 16, I graduate from UC Irvine.

2007   In July, DREAM Act beneficiaries participate in a fast for immigration reform.

In August, I am on a call with Senator Richard Durbin (D-Illinois) and attend training in Washington, DC.

2009   On April 15, I hold the OC Dream Team/DREAMS to be Heard alumni meeting to establish an alliance and rebirth DREAM Team LA.

2010   On April 16, I attend the Reform Immigration for America (RIFA) fundraiser with LA mayor Antonio Villaraigosa, the National Council of La Raza, and movie directors. After they unveil the RIFA campaign, I realize there is still no mention of the DREAM Act or of our efforts; they have no plans to move forward with DREAM as a stand-alone bill.

On May 17, some of my undocumented friends are arrested at John McCain's office and handed over to ICE. It's the first time Dreamers risk deportation for civil disobedience.

On July 20, I am the oldest of nineteen undocumented individuals arrested in Washington for conducting a sit-in inside the Hart Senate Office Building. It is the first time Dreamers are arrested for civil disobedience in the capital. RIFA begins to support DREAM as a stand-alone bill shortly thereafter.

In December, the DREAM Act fails to garner enough support to move forward as a stand-alone bill in the U.S. Senate.

2011   In January, the California Dream Team Alliance and Dream Activist reconvene to discuss alternatives to the passage of the DREAM Act and CIR. We begin researching presidential powers.

In the fall, I move to Iowa.

2012   On June 15, President Obama announces the Deferred Action for Childhood Arrivals (DACA) policy, allowing some undocumented individuals who were brought to the country as children to receive a renewable two-year period of deferred action from deportation and become eligible for a work permit. Eligible recipients cannot have felonies or serious misdemeanors on their records. Unlike the DREAM Act, DACA does not provide a path to citizenship for recipients, known as Dreamers.

On August 10, I approach the American Friends Service Committee (AFSC) to help begin the Iowa DREAM (Act) Coalition.

In September, I apply for DACA.

In October, my daughter Ciel is born prematurely. She spends two and a half months in the hospital.

2013 On January 18, Homeland Security clarifies that DACA recipients have legal presence but no legal status.

On January 22, the Office of the Governor confirms that, based on the memo, granting driver's licenses to DACA recipients does not violate Iowa law.

In March, I end my relationship with my partner and decide to stay in Iowa permanently.

In the summer, my DACA application is approved. I attend events such as a town hall with Charles Grassley (R-Iowa), a leg visit with Tom Latham (R-Iowa), and a walk for immigration reform. I also obtain my first driver's license.

2014 In the summer, I buy my own car.

In November, President Obama announces his intention to expand DACA to cover additional illegal immigrants via Deferred Action for Parents of Americans and Lawful Permanent Residents (DAPA). Multiple states immediately sue to prevent the expansion, which is ultimately blocked by an evenly divided Supreme Court.

2016 On February 1, Ciel and I attend our first political caucus as observers.

In the spring, I buy a house. I am an American homeowner.

On November 8, Donald Trump is elected president. He says he will immediately terminate President Obama's executive order on immigration.

2017   I expect DACA to end on January 20, 2017, so I send in my renewal for DACA on January 7. In the same month, I visit Mama Nina, my grandmother, in Mexico via advance parole, a temporary travel authorization allowing me to reenter the U.S. when I return.

On June 16, President Trump rescinds DAPA (the expansion of DACA) while continuing to review the existence of the program as a whole.

On September 5, the Trump administration rescinds DACA, removing protection for all current and future DACA holders. Implementation is put on hold for six months to allow Congress time to pass the DREAM Act or some other legislative protection for Dreamers. Congress fails to act within the following six months, but multiple states sue to keep DACA in place. No new applicants are allowed, but renewals are accepted while the cases make their way through the courts. I am a survivor and know how to survive without a permit that allows me to work and drive in this country, but I know the challenge. I worry about the kids who qualified for DACA but who might never be able to apply, for my daughter and for the little home that I have built. At the same time, I feel hope that maybe now the Iowa Dreamers will not take DACA for granted, that those affected will wake up and lead the movement.

In October, Mama Nina passes away. I am unable to visit because advance parole is no longer an option.

2018   In April, the Trump administration announces a zero-tolerance policy for immigration, leading to families being separated and children being kept in deplorable conditions in wire mesh compartments (i.e., cages).

In June, President Trump signs an executive order to keep families together after a national outcry. A federal judge orders the administration to reunite those who have been separated; the administration says it may take up to two years to do so.

On October 7, Brett Kavanaugh is sworn as the newest justice of the U.S. Supreme Court, leading to a new conservative majority.

2019 Millions of undocumented immigrants in the U.S. continue to wait for reform and a path to legalization. Of those, nearly 800,000 remain in limbo, awaiting the fate of DACA. I am one of them.

DEAR CIEL

ANTONIA RIVERA

Ciel, my Ciel.

Divine Midwest Child.

Child of the caucus.

Fruit of the resistance.

Learned to love and embrace diversity.

Love is a language that feeds off the radiance of the pores.

It knows no color.

Do not ever tell your kids to drink milk so that your grandchildren will be born a pale white color.

Do not expect to marry someone lighter skinned than you.

Love your neighbor of the South and of the North.

In a way, that is where you began to exist.

Did you know that a woman is born with all the eggs she will need in her lifetime?

You were there when I was an only child, wild and free.

You were there when I used to sing and dance to Cri-Cri.

You were there when I used to wake up with eyes shut with *lagañas* from all the smog in Mexico City.

You were there when I first tasted ketchup.

You were there when I discovered Xuxa.

You were there when I learned to Hula-Hoop, to jump rope and to play handball.

You were there when at six years old, I stopped being a child.

You were there when I took an oath of silence and buried myself in books and television.

You were there when I became a lawyer, a landlord, a banker, a parent, and a negotiator for the men of La Temple.

You were there when I wondered when our journey would end.

When were we going back home to Mexico, when would we get a bed, when would I get my own room, when would we stop moving?

You were there when I wondered when we would stop living among stacked rows of sleeping bodies covering the brown carpet of the apartment.

You waited patiently inside me as an egg until the day you were fertilized.

Your birthday is a very special day.

Do not ever forget that you are an American like your two youngest *tías* and all your cousins.

Remember the strong woman you are tied to.

When it comes time to pursue your passion, think bigger than a doctor or a lawyer.

Know that you can launch a startup.

Know that you can hold public office.

Know that you can become president.

Know that you have the right to pursue life, liberty, and happiness.

QUERIDA CIEL

ANTONIA RIVERA
TRADUCCIÓN AL ESPAÑOL POR NIEVES MARTÍN LÓPEZ

Ciel, mi Ciel.

Hija divina del Midwest.

Hija del registro electoral.

Fruto de la resistencia.

Criada para amar y abrazar la diversidad.

El amor es un lenguaje que se alimenta de la energía que irradian nuestros poros.

No sabe de colores.

Nunca le digas a tus hijos que beban leche para que tus nietos nazcan del mismo pálido color.

No esperes que se casen con alguien de piel más clara que la tuya.

Ama a tu prójimo, al del norte y al del sur.

En cierto modo, ahí comenzó tu existencia.

¿Sabías que una mujer nace con todos los óvulos que necesitará en su vida?

Ya estabas ahí cuando yo era solo una niña libre y salvaje.

Estabas ahí cuando cantaba y bailaba al son de Cri-cri.

Estabas ahí cuando me despertaba con ojos llenos de lagañas por el aire contaminado de la Ciudad de México.

Estabas ahí cuando probé el kétchup por primera vez.

Estabas ahí cuando descubrí a Xuxa.

Estabas ahí cuando aprendí a bailar hula-hoop, a saltar la cuerda y a jugar al balonmano.

Estabas ahí cuando, apenas a los seis años, dejé de ser una niña.

Estabas ahí cuando tomé un voto de silencio y me perdí entre los libros y la televisión.

Estabas ahí cuando me hice abogada, casera, banquera, madre, y negociadora para los hombres de La Temple.

Estabas ahí cuando me preguntaba cuándo terminaría nuestro viaje. Cuándo podríamos volver a México, cuándo podríamos conseguir una cama, mi propia habitación, ¿cuándo dejaríamos de mudarnos?

Estabas ahí cuando me preguntaba cuándo dejaríamos de vivir entre cuerpos y cuerpos juntos, dormidos, cubriendo toda la moqueta marrón del apartamento.

Esperabas pacientemente dentro de mí, ahí en el óvulo, al día en que fueras concebida.

Tu cumpleaños es un día muy especial.

No olvides que eres tan americana como tus tías más jóvenes y todos tus primos.

Recuerda a esta mujer fuerte que te une a ella.

Cuando llegue la hora de perseguir tu pasión, piensa en algo más grande que convertirte en médica o abogada.

Has de saber que puedes crear tu propio negocio.

Has de saber que puedes acceder a un cargo público.

Has de saber que puedes convertirte en presidenta.

Has de saber que tienes derecho a perseguir aquello que te dé vida, libertad y felicidad.

AJLA DIZDAREVIĆ

ARTIST STATEMENT

AS A BOSNIAN AMERICAN, exploring and charting the past is important to me. My parents come from Bosnia, a country that used to be part of Yugoslavia. After Yugoslavia fell into civil war that escalated into genocide, my parents left the country with only a few material objects in their possession. Once they were resettled in the United States, I was born. Years after that, I began to write.

I write not only to unravel the tangled histories of my family but also to validate the multiplicities of my own story as a first-generation American. As the weight of my family's history inevitably shapes me in ways ranging from the benign to the insidious, I am left with scattered pieces of multiple narratives, trying to construct a patchwork attempt at coherence only after facing what has pushed me into the place where I exist as hybrid: Bosnian Lite™, diluted American.

I write to preserve images I've never seen, to freeze collective memories like bugs in amber. I write to resuscitate something that never breathed its truths to me but whose truths were relayed nonetheless. I write in hopes of bringing back to life a home that has faded out of my bloodline by now but that feels cautiously close. There is no sadness in me saying this, just certainty.

A DRINK TO END ALL DRINKS

AJLA DIZDAREVIĆ

The heart said to me, "They've insulted you, they've dragged you through shit. Go on and get drunk, Venichka, go on and get drunk as a skunk." This is what my beautiful heart said.

—Venedikt Erofeev, Moscow to the End of the Line

MY MOTHER used to soak my socks in potent brandy, making sure they were drenched before pulling them over my cold feet, my frozen toes untouched by the fever setting fire to the rest of my body. Even through my stuffed nose, I could smell the strong, fruity *rakija* working to cool me down. "Better than Tylenol," my mother would say knowingly before recorking the bottle and hiding it away in the basement. Years later, I'd creep downstairs barefoot, stopping in front of the shelf displaying my parents' alcohol, face to face with a bottle of Bosnian medicine. The taste of it was atrocious, burning my throat the way the fever had years ago. But still, I drank.

They say when immigrants come to America, language is the first thing to go, food and drink being the last. Assimilate, assimilate, but let the children be real Bosnians by letting them drink. Let them have at least that.

Words that used to flow like the Drina now struggle to leave my mouth. I have to think before I speak, the conjugations failing to come to mind, my imperfect pronunciations embarrassing me, a forgotten word causing me to falter. It is more shameful to be an English speaker than a drunk in our households.

With every war, a culture dies. For us, it was the culture of staying sober for longer than a day. To survive the cruelty of the Ottomans, the ruthlessness of the Nazis, the betrayal of the Serbs, and still be here is nothing short of a miracle. We have endured; we are here. Red-faced and falling over ourselves with the smell of brew on our collars, but here nonetheless. Is our continual existence a testament to our resolve? Or evidence of how we've become the biggest joke in history, a species bumbling its way through every war, surviving by its own dumb luck, washing the taste of humiliation out of its mouth with a little *rakija*?

⁓

Like cigarette smoke that has seeped into the walls, the war will never leave us.

⁓

It's a tale as old as time: *babo* drinks to forget, *sin* drinks to remember, to *feel* something from before the war, from a homeland long gone and never known. Regret versus falsified nostalgia. Sorrow versus romanticism of something never experienced. Looking back to the past inside your heart to find some glimmer of hope for the future always beats not thinking about it at all. To make it sound any better or worse or any more complicated or simple would be a fabrication. Every Bosnian knows drenching a child's socks in brandy brings down a fever. But does it heal a soul? Will it make something ugly sound like poetry? Can it bring a country back to life?

⁓

It ends as it always does, with the child of broken people filling up a cup held in his antsy hands, the liquor fermenting until he grows old enough to lift the cursed drink and take that first sip. Not a brew rich with sugar and cream, but a bitter drink, obscene in the way it sours a voice. Words from the Motherland stop at the roof of a dry mouth, but at least he has this. A clenched jaw, a hard gulp, and, as always, looking forward to nothing at the bottom of the glass.

ŠTA DA VAM KAŽEM

AJLA DIZDAREVIĆ

They had been seated in the back row,

no reclining space on the voyage to the place

where the web of their tongues would be cut,

leaving hanging frenula

to flap at hybrid American babies;

but how could they have known,

once plane touched tarmac

and fragments of old life

were jostled around in plastic bags,

what couldn't be dug up from packed dirt

dressed up as fields?

WHAT CAN I TELL YOU

AJLA DIZDAREVIĆ
PREVEO NA BOSANSKI SULEJMAN DIZDAREVIĆ

Smjestili su ih u neudobna avionska sjedišta u zadnjem redu

na njihovom putovanju ka mjestu

gdje će korijeni njihovih jezika biti odsječeni,

ostavljajući viseći frenulum da se klati

u hibridnim američkim bebama;

ali kako su oni tada mogli znati,

u trenutku dok je avion dodirivao betonsku pist,

šta će da razotkrije tvrdo nabijena crna zemlja

ispod nagizdanih polja

dok su fragmenti starog života bili

razbacani naokolo u plastičnim IOM vrećicama?

HIEU PHAM

ARTIST STATEMENT

I GREW UP feeling untethered from a sense of community. I was a child who had lost her roots, as the Vietnamese adults around me observed, not unkindly but also not entirely accurately. I didn't realize then how my history was connected to the story of other Vietnamese in the diaspora, which is defined by dispossession and displacement. We were all rootless or uprooted to some degree.

I was born in Mỹ Tho, a small city along the Mekong River in southern Vietnam. When I was one year old, my parents and two uncles snuck out of the country by boat and embarked on a seven-day journey across the South China Sea, where we landed in Malaysia and later relocated to another camp in the Philippines. Our final destination was Des Moines, Iowa.

I grew up in Iowa's capital city, with memories of playgrounds on concrete and endless strip malls. Tucked much deeper are sensory memories from the camps—murmurings of adult conversations in twilight hours, the feeling of cool dirt on bare feet. Like many other children from refugee and immigrant communities, I struggled with questions: Who am I? Where do I belong? And why is my self-perception different from how others seem to view and treat me?

What also connects me to other Vietnamese, along with people of all marginalized communities, are the experiences of racism, classism, and for some, colonialism. For these reasons I am interested in people whose stories have not been told, or worse, have been written inaccurately by someone else.

I no longer feel untethered. Culture is transmutable. Our collective memories, rendered into stories, refuse oblivion. I am grateful for the opportunity to tell my own story through the Bicultural Iowa Writers' Fellowship.

WHAT WE OWE OUR MOTHERS

HIEU PHAM

AT 7 A.M. I could already smell the pungent aroma of salted fish. I heard the sizzle and pop of oil in a frying pan. I knew my mother would soon walk upstairs to place a tray of food on my bed, where I had lain for a week since the emergency C-section. "You better not get up, or you'll regret it when you're old," she said, which is what she said yesterday and the day before, scolding me before I'd even disobeyed her.

For a Vietnamese mother, scolding and nagging are part of the mother–child relationship upkeep, a reminder that your mother cares for you and wants you to be the best you can be. The background music to my childhood was a refrain of threats, colloquial life-coaching, and refugee-parent affirmations: "Never pay full price" . . . "Don't go outside in the cold with wet hair" . . . "Don't be too picky about choosing a husband or you'll end up settling for a lesser one." For me and many other children of Asian immigrants and refugees, adolescence and young adulthood were marked by a severe and strangely temporary physical impairment: deafness.

It did cross my mind as I suffered the waves of contractions that I should have listened to my mother, who told me it was best not to wait until my thirties to have children. "You will have a harder time giving birth when you're older," she would say, punctuating a lecture about straightening out my priorities and finally getting married. "I am trying to save you from dying!" My mother uses melodrama as a verbal exclamation mark whenever she thinks one of her children is not listening.

This is the principal drama of Asian immigrant and refugee life, marked by parental sacrifice and ungrateful children. I hope I don't sound bitter, an emotion that pervades many narratives by first-

and second-generation Asian-American children. The resentment is rooted in the perception of having an unpayable filial debt, and it's complicated, whether our parents bequeathed this burden or whether obligation and indebtedness are ingrained in the cultural language we speak.

This filial debt comes with a 500-percent annual interest if you are also a child of refugees. When my mother was twenty years old, she broke a generational cycle of poverty and changed my destiny by persuading my father onto a fishing boat and bringing me, then a toddler, along for the harrowing seven-day journey that brought us to the shores of Malaysia and later the cornfields of Iowa. What was I doing at twenty? I think I was having debates with my college roommate about whether or not short women should wear capris.

The truth is that I hid from my mother's all-seeing eyes for much of my adult life, until I had to return because no one else was seeing me when I needed to be seen. The teenager who decried her assessing gaze because it was always looking for problems—my hair was too oily or my shirt was unflattering—now needed her diligent focus on imperfection in order to feel rested and human following twenty-eight hours of labor that ended in an emergency C-section.

After I came home from the hospital, my mother cooked three meals a day. No shrimp or other shellfish because that will cause inflammation. No chicken, according to Di Sau, or Aunt Six, but I don't remember the reason and never pursued it considering she also warned me against speaking as a protective measure. No showering because of the incision and because of an old Vietnamese practice of keeping recuperating mothers in bed for months until they were properly healed. And twice a day my mother filled an empty wine bottle with hot water before wrapping it in a towel so I could roll it over my swollen stomach. Like a stern nurse, she waited several minutes to be certain I was using the bottle properly before leaving to tend to the rest of her chores. When my fingers accidently touched a piece of glass, I yelped at the intense heat and wondered how my mother avoided scalding herself.

She also harped after my husband to be useful, much to my private amusement. After years of bringing home white men to whom language erected barriers, I married a Vietnamese man to whom she could speak freely. I felt a little bad for him, though, because it seemed as if I had left him behind after the birth of our child. I became a mother in the active sense of the word immediately after my daughter was born, entering what seemed to be a venerable club. Meanwhile, his road to fatherhood was tentative, delayed by the formidable chorale of sisters, cousins, aunties, mother, and mother-in-law surrounding me during the first weeks after I gave birth. We had entered our marriage as a couple united against the colloquial wisdom of our relatives, but these days I was pinching my nose and slurping fatty pork-knuckle broth to stimulate greater breast milk.

When it came to the battle of usefulness, my husband didn't stand a chance next to my mother. She even fought with me about who would stay up to feed the baby. "Let me stay up so you can sleep," she said, but I refused.

One would think I would say "Thank you," but it was difficult to articulate gratitude. Children of refugees resist our parents' advice but live in awe of the magnitude of their sacrifice, keenly aware that they endured struggles we cannot comprehend. Similarly inarticulate, my mother's ministrations of care were executed without softness or sentimentality, only in that terse, pragmatic manner that I'd come to appreciate more than any "I love you." This realization came during the arduous weeks after the birth of my daughter, when I developed an infection from breastfeeding and other complications resulting from labor. At first I resisted my mother's obtrusiveness with the stubbornness of a firstborn daughter, determined to suffer alone and take care of myself.

"Of course, of course. You don't need anyone," my mother said.

I wanted to tell her how that wasn't true. For the first time in my life I wasn't afraid of accumulating more filial debt—I just wanted her by my side to care for me as no one else would, and most importantly, to teach me how to be a mother.

Holding my daughter in those twilight hours, I knew my love would never be articulated in such a profound way. I contemplated how sad it was that she would never remember this moment, when love wasn't demonstrated through words but through my will to be the one solely responsible for taking care of her. She was my child and my obligation, and that wasn't a burden at all.

I wondered if my mother was introduced to motherhood in the same way. I wondered how tired she felt when she held me at her breast. How difficult was it to tend to me when she didn't have enough food to feed herself? How did she find the strength to care for me, to care for all of us, when we were refugees cramped on a fishing boat, floating across the South China Sea?

I could hear my husband at the door. "Do you need anything?" he said.

"Can you get my mother?"

NHỮNG ĐIỀU CHÚNG TA NỢ MẸ MÌNH

HIEU PHAM

ĐƯỢC DỊCH SANG TIẾNG VIỆT BỞI PHUNG NGUYEN

VÀO LÚC 7 GIỜ SÁNG, tôi đã có thể ngửi thấy mùi hăng của cá muối. Tôi nghe thấy tiếng xèo xèo và tiếng dầu nổ trong chảo rán. Tôi biết chắc mẹ tôi sẽ sắp sửa đi lên cầu thang để đặt khay thức ăn trên giường của tôi, nơi tôi đã nằm mẹp suốt một tuần kể từ sau khi sinh mổ khẩn cấp. "Con không nên ngồi dậy, nếu không con sẽ hối hận khi về già," mẹ đã nói vậy, đó là những gì mẹ đã nói hôm qua và hôm kia, thậm chí mắng tôi trước khi tôi không nghe lời của mẹ.

Đối với một người mẹ Việt Nam, la mắng và cần nhằn là một cách thể hiện tình yêu thương của mẹ đối với con cái, đó là một sự nhắc nhở rằng mẹ luôn quan tâm đến bạn và muốn bạn có thể trở thành người tốt nhất. Như một loại nhạc nền trong thời thơ ấu của tôi là một sự kiềm chế bằng sự răn đe, huấn luyện cuộc sống theo khuôn khổ và khẳng định tính cách của cha mẹ tị nạn: "Không được trả nguyên giá" ... "Đừng đi ra ngoài trời lạnh với mái tóc ướt" ... "Đừng có kén cá chọn canh rồi cuối cùng lại gặp phải người không ra gì". Đối với tôi và nhiều đứa trẻ khác của người di dân và người tị nạn châu Á, cái tuổi mới lớn và tuổi thanh niên bị đánh dấu bởi một khiếm khuyết thể chất nghiêm trọng và kỳ lạ: điếc.

Nó tái hiện lại trong tâm thức tôi khi tôi phải chịu đựng những cơn chuyển dạ mà đáng lẽ tôi phải nghe lời mẹ, người đã nói với tôi rằng tốt nhất là đừng đợi đến năm ba mươi mới có con. "Càng lớn tuổi sinh nở càng khó", mẹ tôi nói vậy, nhấn từng câu trong bài lên lớp trong việc sửa lưng tôi về trách nhiệm và nghĩa vụ của tôi và cuối cùng là việc lập gia đình. "Mẹ đang cố gắng cứu mạng con đấy!" Mẹ tôi sử dụng sự cường điệu như một dấu chấm than bằng lời nói bất cứ khi nào mẹ nghĩ rằng một trong những đứa con của mình không chịu lắng nghe.

Đây là một vở kịch chính về cuộc sống di dân và ty nạn của người Á Châu, được đánh dấu bằng sự hy sinh của cha mẹ và những đứa con vô ơn. Tôi hy vọng rằng tôi đã không tỏ vẻ chua chát, một cảm xúc bao trùm nhiều câu chuyện kể của những đứa trẻ Mỹ gốc Á ở thế hệ thứ nhất và thứ hai. Sự cay đắng bắt nguồn từ nhận thức về việc có một khoản nợ hiếu thảo không thể trả được, và nó phức tạp, cho dù cha mẹ chúng ta có gánh chịu gánh nặng này hay là sự ràng buộc hoặc và ngập nợ đã ăn sâu vào ngôn ngữ chúng ta thường dùng.

Khoản nợ hiếu thảo này đi kèm với lãi suất hàng năm 500 phần trăm nếu bạn cũng là đứa con của người tị nạn. Năm mẹ tôi hai mươi tuổi, bà đã phá vỡ sự nghèo khổ truyền kiếp và thay đổi vận mệnh của tôi bằng cách thuyết phục cha tôi lên một chiếc thuyền đánh cá và mang tôi theo, khi đó chỉ là một đứa trẻ mới biết đi, trong hành trình bảy ngày đầy gian nan đưa chúng tôi đến bờ biển của Malaysia và sau đó là cánh đồng ngô bạt ngàn của tiểu bang Iowa. Tôi đã làm gì ở tuổi hai mươi? Tôi nghĩ rằng tôi đã có những cuộc tranh luận với bạn đại học sống chung cùng phòng về việc phụ nữ có nên mặc quần lửng hay không.

Sự thật là tôi đã trốn tránh sự quản thúc của mẹ tôi trong suốt thời gian trưởng thành của mình, cho đến khi tôi phải trở về nhà, vì không ai hiểu được tôi khi tôi cần được hiểu. Một người thiếu nữ đã tránh né những cái nhìn xét nét của mẹ cô ấy, vì mẹ cô luôn tìm ra những điểm không hoàn hảo về cô như là tóc của cô thì quá nhiều dầu, áo của cô không được ủi thẳng-giờ cô ấy lại nhận ra mình cần sự quan tâm, tỉ mỉ của mẹ để phát hiện ra những điều không hoàn hảo ấy, để cô có thể được nghỉ ngơi và tự tại sau khi trải qua hai mươi tám giờ chuyển dạ khi sinh mổ khẩn cấp.

Sau khi tôi từ bệnh viện về nhà, mẹ tôi nấu ba bữa ăn trong một ngày. Không tôm, không sò ốc vì sẽ làm sưng vết thương. Không được ăn gà, theo lời Di Sau, hay Dì Sáu, nhưng tôi không nhớ lý do và không bao giờ quan tâm lắm, và dì cũng cảnh cáo tôi không được cãi lại những lời nói vì đó như một biện pháp bảo vệ. Không được tắm vì vết mổ và vì một tập tục của người Việt là ở cữ nhiều tháng sau sanh cho đến khi vết thương lành hẳn. Và ngày hai lần mẹ tôi đổ đầy nước nóng vào vỏ một chai rượu đã dùng hết, quấn nó vào một chiếc khăn để tôi có thể lăn nó trên cái bụng sưng phồng của tôi. Giống như một y tá nghiêm khắc, bà chờ đợi vài phút để chắc rằng tôi lăn chai nước đứng cách trước khi rời đi để lo những phần công việc còn lại của bà. Khi những ngón tay của tôi vô tình chạm vào vỏ chai, tôi thét lên vì sức nóng dữ dội và tự hỏi làm thế nào mẹ tôi tránh được việc tự gây phỏng cho bà.

Bà cũng cằm ràm chồng tôi phải biết giúp vợ những việc có ích, những giây phút đó, tôi cảm thấy thú vị và hài hước, nhưng tôi chỉ giữ trong lòng. Sau nhiều năm dắt về nhà những người đàn ông da trắng mà ngôn ngữ là những rào cản, rồi thì tôi cũng kết hôn với một người đàn ông Việt Nam mà bà có thể nói chuyện huyên thuyên, thỏa thích. Mặc dù vậy, tôi cảm thấy tội nghiệp cho chồng tôi, vì dường như tôi đã chẳng màng đến anh ấy lại sau khi con chúng tôi ra đời. Tôi trở thành một người mẹ bận rộn đúng nghĩa ngày sau khi sinh bé gái, giống như được gia nhập vào một câu lạc bộ hạng sang. Trong khi đó, con đường trở thành người cha của chồng tôi xem chừng bị chững lại, bị trì hoãn bởi một mớ âm thanh hỗn độn của chị em, anh em họ, dì, mẹ và mẹ chồng bao quanh tôi trong những tuần lễ đầu tiên sau khi sanh con. Chúng tôi đã bước vào sự hôn nhân giống như một đôi vợ chồng hợp nhất chống lại những quan niệm cổ hủ của bà con họ hàng chúng tôi, nhưng những ngày này, tôi phải bịt mũi để húp đại súp giò heo để có sữa cho con bú.

Khi phải tranh luận về những điều có ích, chồng tôi cũng không còn cơ hội đứng về phía mẹ. Thậm chí bà còn giành với tôi về việc ai sẽ thức đêm để cho em bé bú. Mẹ nói: "Để mẹ thức cho con ngủ," nhưng tôi từ chối.

Mọi người nghĩ tôi sẽ nói lời "Cám ơn," nhưng thật khó để nói lên lòng biết ơn. Con cái của những người tị nạn cãi lại lời khuyên của cha mẹ mình, nhưng sống trong sự nể phục về sự hy sinh to lớn của họ, nhận thức sâu sắc rằng họ cam chịu bền bỉ mà chúng tôi không thể hiểu được thấu đáo. Tương tự như vậy, sự chăm sóc tận tụy của mẹ tôi được thể hiện không vì sự yếu đuối hay ủy mị, mà là sự ngắn gọn, thực tiễn mà tôi tỏ lòng biết ơn hơn là nói suông "con thương mẹ". Sự nhận thức đến trong những tuần lễ vật vã sau khi sinh bé gái, khi ngực tôi bị sưng tấy do cho con bú và các triệu chứng phiền toái khác do sự sinh nở. Lúc đầu, tôi phản đối sự quấy rầy của mẹ về sự sinh khó con gái đầu lòng của tôi, tôi muốn tự mình chịu đựng và lo liệu lấy bản thân.

"Tất nhiên, tất nhiên rồi. Con không cần ai hết," mẹ tôi nói vậy.

Tôi muốn nói với mẹ rằng ý tôi không phải như vậy. Lần đầu tiên trong đời, tôi đã không ngại mắc thêm món nợ ơn nghĩa, tôi chỉ muốn có mẹ bên cạnh chăm sóc tôi mà không người nào khác, và điều quan trọng nhất là dạy tôi cách làm mẹ.

Bế con gái tôi trong căn phòng lờ mờ, tôi biết tình thương của tôi sẽ không bao giờ được biểu lộ một cách sâu sắc như vậy. Tôi ngẫm nghĩ rằng bé sẽ không bao giờ nhớ được khoảnh khắc này, khi tình yêu thương không được thể hiện bằng lời, nhưng qua sự ước muốn tôi là người duy nhất có trách nhiệm chăm sóc con tôi. Bé là con tôi và là bổn phận làm mẹ của tôi, và đó không phải là gánh nặng.

Tôi tự hỏi không biết mẹ tôi bước vào cuộc sống làm mẹ có giống tôi không. Tôi tự hỏi mẹ đã mệt mỏi thế nào khi ôm tôi vào lòng. Những khó khăn vất vả nuôi tôi ngay cả khi mẹ không có đủ thực phẩm để ăn? Làm sao mẹ có đủ sức mạnh để chăm sóc tôi, chăm sóc tất cả chị em chúng tôi, khi tất cả chúng tôi là những người tị nạn chen chúc nhau trên một chiếc thuyền nhỏ trôi nổi trên Biển Đông?

Tôi nghe tiếng chồng tôi nói vọng vào ở cửa. "Em có cần gì không?"

"Anh gọi mẹ giúp em?"

84

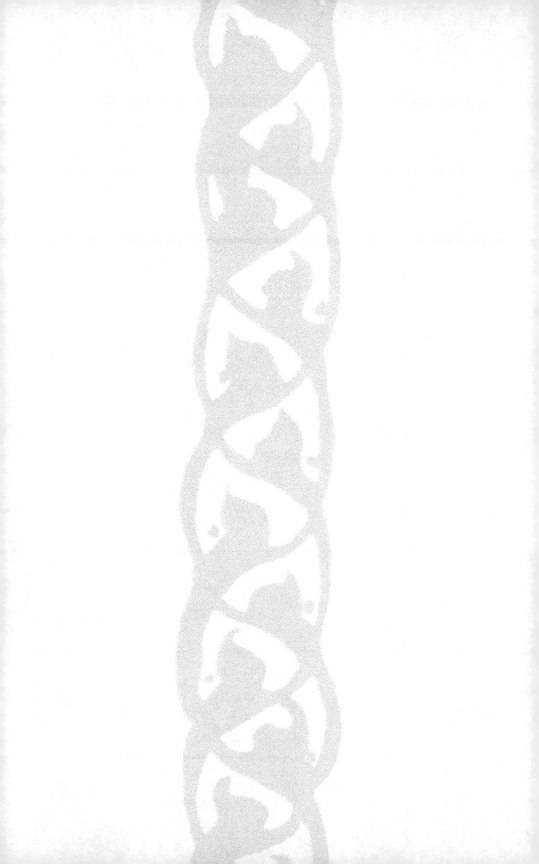

SARAH ELGATIAN

ARTIST STATEMENT

THE ONE FACT *I never questioned about my identity was that I am Armenian, but the vast majority of Armenians I know are family members. When I visited Los Angeles for a writing conference in 2016, I found myself surrounded by Armenian stories. I felt a deep connection with these people from my lineage, but I also felt painfully removed from the culture everyone else seemed to understand intrinsically.*

This essay was written in pieces as I tried to parse out my place in the Armenian culture I so revered: sometimes it was a letter to my grandmother who had died a few years prior, sometimes it was a statement of identity. It has been in my heart for my entire life, and it was a painful, difficult process to get it out. I sobbed through lectures and panels in LA, and I cried during every iteration of this story. More than anything, I kept finding that I had more questions than I would ever be able to answer. I kept finding that my grandparents hid their stories from everyone around them. The more research I do, the more at a loss I feel. But then, the more I learn about Armenia, the closer I feel to it. In writing this essay I made definite plans to visit, finally. I am terrified—I won't have a tour guide and I don't speak the language— but I also feel like at last I'm coming upon something right.

A NEW DIASPORA

SARAH ELGATIAN

ANNIG HAD A FACE like a knotted tree. You could hear dust on her tongue when she spoke, and she spoke like a crow—flat and shrill and always half yelling. Her life was built like a folktale, with poverty, war, running for her life, refugees, exotic islands, and a mail-order marriage to a man she didn't know. She held a country between her shoulders and ten children in her womb. A life of survival taught her mind over matter in all things. Her morning sickness she treated by playing cards. Her hunger she treated by turning rocks into dice.

I remember her in her small kitchen shaped like a crooked *L*. She had three chairs at a lopsided table covered by a clear plastic sheet and a pile of junk mail. One chair was in a corner blocked off by a counter, another was in the way of the walking space, and the third nearly touched the front door when pulled out. This is where Annig sat and shuffled cards and drank tiny cups of thick coffee.

Annig was Armenian, a survivor, who was born during a genocide, learned to read and write at a refugee camp in Syria, and came of age in Batista's Cuba. She had browned olive skin; thick, coarse black hair; and an undisguisable accent. But I only knew her seated in that chair by the door with a demitasse tilted toward her and a stack of frayed red-backed playing cards in front of her.

Grandma Annig refused to speak English. She'd sooner speak Spanish to her grandchildren than say anything but insults in their native language. She spoke English fine through her thick accent at the corner store or with the neighbors but never with her family. I can respect that now, though I never learned Armenian or Spanish. So we'd sit around her tiny table and play the only game she knew how to play: Crazy Eights. Grandma cheated, cackling with her empty mouth wide when we had to draw great stores of cards and

89

when her hand emptied. She was not kind and she did not like jokes.

Survivors of genocide are not soft people. They are not warm and welcoming. Trauma did not create cookie-baking, blanket-knitting grandmothers. Annig accepted nothing short of perfection, and we were terrified of the venom that came through her frantic foreign yells. She didn't share stories or dessert with her grandchildren, but she did love us. We didn't understand it, of course, but it was all she had to give.

She tried to teach me Armenian from an ancient workbook she'd used to learn English while stranded in Cuba during her fourteen-year layover between Armenia and the United States. She brought photo albums to the kitchen full of delicate, poorly colored photographs of her in her youth, wearing a stiff, tea-length ivory dress, hair carefully coiffed. These, I suspect, were the photos used to sell her to the first Armenian in America who could pay her passage to Ellis Island. Many men, she told me, proposed marriage to her in Cuba, but she was the oldest sibling and she had to bring her family to America.

After the first time I finished the food she put in front of me—grilled cheese made in what I called a "sandwich maker" for twenty years—she started making it as soon as I arrived at her house. She also bullied me about my squinty eyes. "Can you see, Zarahoui? Where you eyes? You blind?" My eyes are tiny anime half-moons identical to her own. She grabbed my nose in tight pinches and cackled, "You lie? Pinocchio? You smell California?" The knob between her knuckles mirrored the drooping nose of her youth. My faint mustache and the dark circles under my eyes matched hers, and she mocked them relentlessly. Thrilled when I ate her food, she called me fat and took a handful of my potbelly.

This kind of love is not obvious to children, but it is love. It is love like armor, and so I don't want to deny my grandmother when people look at me. Her children were embarrassed by their dark skin and their poverty and their parents' thick accents. They changed the way they pronounced their last name. They called themselves Eastern European. They learned to eat canned vegetables and drink soda. They married blond hair and blue eyes without exception.

Every step closer to "normal" was a step closer to forgetting.

Only one of my cousins could speak to my grandma, and she was born with her father's coloring—blond and blue. Her skin is darker than his, but I wonder: Does she feel the way I do? Growing up in Iowa, the only people who looked like my grandparents were related to me. No one else had dark skin, coarse black hair, or a nose like a bird of prey. My dad let people assign his ethnicity to him. At the family restaurant he was Greek; at the pizza place he was Italian. There was one Lebanese woman, whose husband was white and worked at John Deere, who likely still believes my family is from Lebanon. My dad shared his office with a Mexican woman for two years who sometimes spoke Spanish to him.

I don't want to do that. I want to own my grandmother's squiggly alphabet and quit tweezing my face. I want to tell my uncle who fears Syrian refugees that those same Syrians gave his parents refuge. I want to see the mountain prominently displayed in every Armenian's home and call it my own.

I had no concept of Mount Ararat's importance or cruel symbolism when I first saw Armenia on a map. I only knew it as the centerpiece of Armenian homes: a painting of Big Ararat and Little Ararat cuddling against a perfect blue sky. I got excited when the news anchor gestured toward the region. Then he said, "war," "terrorism," "oil." The Near East, it turned out, was not everyone's mantelpiece paradise. My whiteness may be the greatest gift my father ever gave me, but it feels like a lie. Dad said his family was from "part of the former Soviet Union." He said "Mediterranean." He gets stopped at airports.

I always thought assimilation was akin to lying. I failed to recognize the survival skills my father inherited from his parents. My grandfather, during a long march from one death camp to another, collapsed, skeletal, in the desert and was left for dead. Who was he to correct them? Who was I to tell my father to call his homeland the Middle East if careful phrasing kept him safe?

Still, it's taken work to uncover the culture Annig carried with her when she could carry nothing else. I feel an emptiness in my stomach and a block in my throat when I realize I will never have answers. I don't know how my grandparents survived, only that they valued survival above all else. I'm afraid to ask my cousins if they feel as lost, off-white, and hungry as I do. I can't ask because it doesn't matter; we can't get our culture back. I feel my grandmother's mountain, her cross, her thirty-six-letter alphabet in my heart, but I have no access to them.

When I go someday to Armenia with my light hair and pink cheeks, I will tell the natives I'm one of them and pray they tell me what it means. It's a cruel century-long joke that has created this new diaspora: here we struggle to gather, thirsting for our grandparents and their stories, white-washed, tongueless, and unable to make pilaf. We search anxiously in movie credits and on maps for a sign of our people, holding Raffi, Cher, System of a Down, the Kardashians close to our hearts, scared to have white children who won't know the resilience in their blood.

But we go back. We hang paintings of Ararat over our own mantels, and we read fortunes from coffee grounds. We trade recipes with cousins and forward news stories about chess champions and rebellion. I am not alone in taking pride in coming from a people whose whole history is of grit, art, and survival, but this awe that burns inside me doesn't mean I'm Armenian enough. Rumor has it that you're not really Armenian if you don't speak the language. I don't. But I keep that mountain always in my sight.

ՆՈՐ ՍՓՅՈՒՌՔԸ

SARAH ELGATIAN
ԹԱՐԳՄԱՆՎԱԾ Է ՀԱՅԵՐԵՆ ԼԻԼԻԹ ՊԵՏՐՈՍՅԱՆ

Անիգի դեմքը կարծես հյուսված ծառլիներ։ Երբ նա խոսում էր, լեզվի վրա լսելի էր դարեր շարունակ կուտակված փոշին, և նա խոսում էր ագռավի պես՝ չոր և սուր, գրեթե գռռալով ։ Նրա կյանքը կարծես ժողովրդական հեքիաթ լիներ, որը լի էր աղքատությամբ ու պատերազմներով, կյանքի գոյատևման պայքարով, փախստականներով, էկզոտիկ կողիներով և պատվերով ամուսնությամբ մի մարդու հետ, որին նա չէր էլ ճանաչում։ Նա իր ուսերին մի ամբողջ երկիր է կրել և իր տասը զավակներին՝ արգանդում։ Գոյատևողի կյանքը նրան ուսուցանել է և տվել մեծ կամքի ուժ ամեն հարցում։ Առավոտվա հիվանդությունը նա բուժում էր խաղաթղթերով ։ Քաղցը՝ բուժում էր զառախաղով։

Ես հիշում եմ նրան իր փոքրիկ խոհանոցում, որը ծռված L-ի տեսք ուներ ։ Նա ուներ երեք աթոռ, թեք մի սեղան, որը ծածկված էր թափանցիկ մոմլաթե ծածկոցով և գվազդային թերթերի կույտով։ Մեկ աթոռը մի անկյունում արգելափակված էր, մյուսը՝ երբ օգտագործվում էր, սեղակի մեջտեղում էր հայտնվում, իսկ երրորդ աթոռը գրեթե հավում էր մուտքի դռանը երբ դուրս էր քաշված։ Ահա այստեղ էլ Անիգը նստում էր ու խառնում իր խաղաքարտերը և իմում էր փոքրիկ բաժակով թունդ սուրճը։

Անիգը (Աի Նիգ) հայ էր, ցեղասպանության տարիներին ծնված և մազապուրծ եղած, նա կարդալ և գրել սովորել էր Սիրիայում՝ փախստականների ճամբարում, և մեծացել էր բատիստյան Կուբայում։ Նա ուներ շագանակագույն ձիթապտղի մաշկ, խիտ կոպիտ

93

սև մազեր և անքողարկելի ակցենտ: Բայց ես նրան միայն ճանաչել եմ դռան մոտ տեղադրված այդ աթոռին նստած, գավաթը կես չափով դեպի իրեն շրջած և ճմրթված կարմիր խաղաքարտերի կույտը դիմացը դրված:

Անիգ տատիկը հրաժարվում էր խոսել անգլերեն: Նա ավելի շուտ իսպաներեն էր խոսում իր թոռների հետ, քան թե որևէ այլ բան ասում բացի հայհոյանքներից մայրենի լեզվով: Նա անգլերեն լեզվով լավ էր խոսում իր կոպիտ ակցենտով անկյունի խանութում կամ հարևանների հետ, բայց իր ընտանիքի հետ՝ երբեք: Հիմա ես կարող եմ հարցել դա, թեպետ երբեք չեմ սովորել հայերեն կամ իսպաներեն: Այնպես որ, մենք նստում էինք իր փոքրիկ սեղանի շուրջ և խաղում միակ խաղը, որը Անիգը գիտեր, թե ինչպես խաղալ՝ դա ամերիկյան 8եր խաղն էր : (Ես չեմ կատակում, մի անգամ փորձել ենք սովորեցնել նրան Ուևո խաղալ, բայց չստացվեց : Չնայած որ երկուսն էլ գրեթե նույն խաղն են:) Տատիկը խաբեբայություն էր անում: Նա չարախնդորեն բացում էր բերանը, երբ մենք ստիպված էինք մեծ քարտեր քաշել և երբ իր ձեռքը դատարկվում էր: Նա բարի չէր և կատակ չէր սիրում:

Ցեղասպանությունից մազապուրծ եղածները փափկասիրտ մարդիկ չեն: Նրանք ջերմ և հյուրընկալ չեն: Էմոցիոնալ վնասվածքները չեն կերտել բլիթներ թխող, ծածկոց գործող տատիկների: Անիգը ոչինչ կատարյալ չէր ընդունում, և մենք սարսափում էինք այն թույնից, որը հոսում էր իր կատաղած օտարական գործառույցներից: Նա պատմություններ կամ աղանդեր չէր կիսում իր թոռների հետ, բայց նա սիրում էր մեզ: Մենք դա չէինք հասկանում, իհարկե, բայց դա այն ամենն էր, ինչ նա կարող էր տալ:

Նա փորձել է ինձ հայերեն սովորեցնել մի հնավուրց դասագրքով, որը ինքը օգտագործել է անգլերեն սովորելու համար Կուբայում՝ Հայաստանից մինչ Միացյալ Նահանգներ հասնելու երկար ու դիմակայության 14 տարիների ընթացքում: Նա լուսանկարչական ալբոմներ էր բերում խոհանոց, որոնք լի էին Անիգի

94

երիտասարդության տարիների նրբագեղ, գունագրկված լուսանկարներով՝ մազերը խնամքով ձիգ կապված էին, փողոսկրագույն գզեստը իջնում էր մինչ ծնկները: Սրանք, ես կասկած ունեմ, որ այն լուսանկարներն են, որոնք օգտագործվել են նրան վաճառելու Ամերիկայում առաջին պատռահած հային, որը կարող էր վճարել իր անցումը դեպի Էլիս կղզի: Նա պատմում էր ինձ, որ Կուբայում շատ տղամարդիկ իրեն ամուսնության առաջարկ են արել, բայց նա ավագն էր իր քույր - եղբայրների մեջ և պետք է ընտանիքը բերեր Ամերիկա:

Առաջին անգամ, երբ ես ավարտեցի այն ուտեստը, որը նա դրել էր իմ առջև՝ տապակած պանիր, որ ես 20 տարի շարունակ անվանում էի «սենդվիչ պատրաստող», նա սկսեց պատրաստել այն ամեն անգամ՝ հենց գնում էի իր տուն:

Նա անհանգստացնում էր, բորբոքում ու խռովեցնում էր ինձ իմ շեղ աչքերի համար իր կոտրված անգլերենով՝ «Կարո՞դ ես տեսնել, Զարուհի: Որտե՞ղ են քո աչքերը: Դու կու՞յր ես »: Աչքերս փոքրիկ կիսալուսնաձև են, որոնք նման են իր աչքերին: Նա պինդ բռնում էր իմ քիթը մատների արանքում և բարձրաձայն ասում էր ՝« Դու ստու՞մ ես, Պինոքի՞ո, վրայից Կալիֆոռնիայի հո՞տ է փչում» :

Իմ մոտ քիթը, որ նա քաշքշում էր, արտացոլում էր իր երիտասարդության կախ ընկած քիթը: Իմ աննշան բեղիկներն ու աչքերի տակ գտնվող մուգ շրջանակները նման էին իր դեմքին, և նա անիսա ծաղրում էր ինձ դրանց համար: Երջանիկ էր, որ ուտում էի իր պատրաստած ուտելիքը, բայց նա ինձ կշտում էր գեր և բռնում էր փորիս ծալքերը:

Նման սերը ակնհայտ չէր երեխաների համար, բայց դա սեր էր: Դա սեր էր, որ նման էր զենք ու գրահի, և այդ պատճառով ես չեմ ուզում ժիստել տատիկիս, երբ մարդիկ նայում են ինձ: Նրա երեխաները ամաչում էին և՛ իրենց մուգ մաշկի և՛ իրենց աղքատության և՛ ծնողների խիստ ակցենտի համար: Նրանք փորեցին իրենց ազգանունը արտասանելու ձևը: Նրանք իրենց անվանում էին արևելյան եվրոպացիներ: Նրանք սովորեցին ուտել պահածոյացված բանջարեղեն և խմել գազային խմիչքներ: Նրանք, առանց բացառության, ամուսնացան շեկ մազերով և կապույտ աչքերով մարդկանց հետ: Յուրաքանչյուր քայլ դեպի նորմալը, քայլ էր դեպի մոռացություն:

Միայն իմ զարմիկներից մեկը կարող էր խոսել տատիկիս հետ, և նա ծնվել էր իր հոր գույներով՝ շիկահեր և կապույտ աչքերով: Նրա մաշկը ավելի մուգ է քան իր հայրիկինը, բայց հետաքրքիր է, արդյո՞ք նա ունի նույն զգացողությունները, ինչ՝ ես: Այնվայում մեծանալով հասկացա, որ միակ մարդիկ, որոնք նման էին տատիկիս ու պապիկիս իմ հարազատներն էին: Ոչ ոք չուներ մուգ մաշկ, կոպիտ, ալիքաձև սև մազեր կամ անգղի նման քիթ: Հայրս թողնում էր, որ մարդիկ իրեն հատկացնեն իր էթնիկ պատկանելիությունը: Ընտանեկան ռեստորանում նա հույն էր, պիցցայի վայրում՝ իտալացի: Մի լիբանանցի կին կար, որի ամուսինը սպիտակամորթ էր և աշխատում էր Ջոն Դիր ընկերությունում, նա հավանաբար մինչ հիմա հավատում է, որ իմ ընտանիքը Լիբանանից է: Հայրս աշխատում էր գրասենյակում մի մեքսիկացի կնոջ հետ, որը հորս հետ երբեմն իսպաներեն էր խոսում:

Ես չեմ ուզում այդպես անել: Ես ուզում եմ իմ տատիկի ոլոր-մոլոր այբուբենը տիրապետել և այլևս դեմքս չմազահանել: Ես ուզում եմ ասել իմ հորեղբորը, ով վախենում է սիրիացի փախստականներից, որ այդ նույն սիրիացիները ապաստան են տվել իր ծնողներին: Ցանկանում եմ տեսնել ամեն հայի օջախում ակնհայտորեն ցուցադրված սարը, և այն կոչել իմ սեփականը:

Ես Մասիս սարի կամ նրա դաժան խորհրդանիշի մասին գաղափար չունեի, երբ առաջին անգամ տեսա Հայաստանը քարտեզի վրա: Ես միայն գիտեի, որ դա հայերի օրրան է եղել՝ մեծ և փոքր Արարատ լեռները գրկախառնված՝ պարզ կապուտակ երկնքի ֆոնի վրա:

Ես շատ ուրախացա, այն ժամանակ, երբ

հեռուստացույցով լուրերը սկսեցին խոսել տարածաշրջանի մասին: Հետո ասվեց «պատերազմ», «ահաբեկչություն», «նավթ»: Պարզվեց, որ Մերձավոր Արևելքը ոչ բոլորի համար էր դրախտային օջախ: Իմ սպիտակությունը այն մեծագույն պարգևն է, որ երբևէ հայրս տվել է ինձ, բայց կարծես թե կեղծիք լինի: Հայրս ասում էր, որ իր ընտանիքը «Խորհրդային միության» մասն էր կազմում: Երբ նա ասում էր «Միջերկրական»` նրան կանգնեցնում էին օդանավակայանում:

Ես միշտ կարծել եմ, որ հարմարվելը խաբեբայության նման մի բան է: Ես չէի կարող նկատել գոյատևման այդ ունակությունը, որը հայրս ժառանգել էր իր ծնողներից: Պապս մի մահկան ճամբարից մյունը երկար ու անվերջ քայլարշավի ժամանակ տապալվել է գետնին, կմախքի աստիճան հյուծված լինելով` անապատում մնացել է որպես դի: Նա ո՞վ էր, որ դիտողություն աներ նրանց: Ով եմ ես, որ հորս ասեմ, որ իր հայրենիքը կոչի Մերձավոր Արևելք, այն դեպքում, երբ ճիշտ ասված խոսքը ապահովություն է երաշխավորում նրան:

Այնուամենայնիվ, մեծ ջանքեր պահանջվեցին բացահայտելու մշակույթը, որ Անիզը կրում էր իր մեջ, երբ ուրիշ ոչինչ չկար կրելու: Ես դատարկություն եմ զգում ստամոքսումս և մի գունդ կոկորդիս մեջ խցանված, երբ հասկանում եմ, որ երբեք չեմ ունենա պատասխաններ: Ես չգիտեմ, թե ինչպես են իմ տատիկն ու պապիկը գոյատևել, միայն գիտեմ, որ նրանք գոյատևումը ամենից վեր էին դասում: Վախենում եմ հարցնել իմ զարմիկներին, թե արդյոք նրանք նույնքան մոլորված են զգում իրենց, տեղեկության կարոտ, ինչպես ես ինքս: Ես չեմ կարող հարցնել, քանի որ դա նշանակություն չունի այլևս, մենք չենք կարող վերադարձնել մեր մշակույթը: Ես զգում եմ իմ սրտում տատիկիս սարը, նրա խաչը, նրա 36 տառանոց այբուբենը, բայց դրանք ինձ հասանելի չեն:

Երբ ես մի օր գնամ Հայաստան, իմ բաց գույնի մազերով և վարդագույն այտերով, ես տեղաբնակներին կասեմ, որ նրանցից մեկն եմ, ու կաղոթեմ, որ նրանք ինձ բացատրեն, թե դա ինչ է նշանակում: Դարերից

97

Եկած մի կատակ կա, որը ստեղծվել է այս նոր սփյուռքի կողմից՝ այստեղ մենք պայքարում ենք համախմբվելու համար, կարոտ մնալով մեր տատիկ - պապիկներին և նրանց պատմություններին՝ սպիտակամ՞շկ, անլեզու և փլավ սարքել չիմանալով: Մենք անընդհատ փնտրում ենք ֆիլմերի շնորհակալական տողերի մեջ և քարտեզների վրա մեր ժողովրդի մի մասնիկ, մի նշան՝ պահելով Րաֆֆիին, Շերին, Սիսթեմ օֆ ա դաուն խմբին, Քարդաշյանններին մեր սրտին մոտ, սարսափելով այն մտքից, որ սպիտակ երեխաներ կունենաք, ովքեր չեն իմանա իրենց արյան մեջ հոսող դիմակայունությունը:

Բայց մենք վերադառնում ենք: Արարատի նկարները կախում ենք մեր սեփական օջախներում և սուրճի հատակին բախտ ենք կարդում: Մենք մեր զարմիկների հետ բաղադրատոմեր ենք փոխանակում, կիսվում ենք նորություններով և շախմատային չեմպիոնների հաջողություններով, ինչպես նաև ապստամբության մասին նորություններով: Մենակ ես չեմ, որ հպարտանում եմ այն հանգամանքով, որ ծագում ունեմ մի ժողովրդից, որի ամբողջ պատմությունը բաղկացած է կոշտ ու կոպիտ բնավորությունից, արվեստից և գոյատնման պայքարից, բայց այս խորագույն հարցանքը, որ վառվում է ներսումս դեռ չի նշանակում, որ ես բավականաչափ հայ եմ: Ասում են, որ դու իսկական հայ չես, եթե դու չես խոսում լեզուն: Ես չեմ խոսում: Բայց այդ սարը միշտ պահում եմ հիշողությանս մեջ:

98

RANA HEWEZI

ARTIST STATEMENT

I WAS RAISED in commotion: amid the bargaining of vendors and the piercing sidewalk chatter that deafened the greetings from the taxi horn. Cairo was renowned for its distinct perfume of car exhaust compiled with the honeyed breath of freshly prepared basbousa. *At age two, I traded the clamor of Cairo for the muted blare of Paris. I found familiarity in the background noise while consuming the distinct sights of* boulangeries. *When I moved to Ames, Iowa, as a seven-year-old, the distinctive ruckus was replaced with a tranquility that swallowed even the most deafening of noises. I found home in a place that made no display to be seen yet was heard nonetheless.*

I spent my early childhood mastering languages unlike my own Arabic speech—first French, then English. Yet, it took being devoid of words to truly recognize their value. As my words became my own, I began to view expression as a platform that captured my fluid character as I straddled various divergent identities. On paper, I constructed an individual who encountered coherence rather than conformity between her counterparts. Through my writing, I was able to transcend time and space, all within the comforts of my chosen home. My words were able to recite the distinctive adhan *for prayer, indulge my craving for* mousse au chocolat, *and diffuse the natural perfume of an Iowa spring.*

A GATEWAY TO JENNA

RANA HEWEZI

Act like the sunrise; grasp for the light until the darkness is cast away.

They say tears grieve the words that remain hostage to the mind.
A merciful action that allows one to hear what remains unsaid.

In English, *tear* has many meanings.
The first that comes to mind is the salty residue emerging from the eyes.
Yet, I always thought it was interesting that it is also used to describe something that has been ripped.
Or torn.
Generating something that was no longer whole.
Except it was pronounced {*ter*} instead of {*'tir*}.

They were identical in my eyes.

In Arabic, tears is pronounced {*dumueh*}.
It resembles the word *dam*, meaning blood.

‿

Most people are unaware that *Mama* had three siblings.
One had escaped Life's slippery hold in exchange for Death's unwavering clutch.
A brother whose name so often grappled within the periphery

of *Mama's* mouth and innermost thoughts.

A pain she had not chosen to forget yet could not remember.

He, alongside Death, plagued her thoughts.

Issam.

A name that brought a reminder that fragility and humanity were bound like a book to its spine: while the spine established the anchor of the book, it also hindered its resiliency.

Yet, we cannot afford to be liberated pages. From the moment we are born, we are bound to Death. Promised to Him from the onset of our conception and united with Him as we relinquish Life's honeyed breath.

And Death was not sympathetic, for He who only takes cannot learn to give.

‿

Like *Baba*, *Mama* could relate to the tainted deeds shared intimately between Loss and Death.

While *Baba* was raised in the spotlight, *Mama* preferred the security of the shadows.
She grew reserved in fear of Death's impenetrable eyes.

Cautious and innocent.
To attract attention to oneself was to compromise the life that was embezzled from Death's unforgiving hold.

The talk of the community could just as easily be whispered into Death's ears.

There is a common expression in Arabic, advice for escaping the scrutiny of the people:

Imshee gam bel heta.

Walk alongside the wall.

Despite the natural push toward deference as a woman, everything in *Mama's* nature went against that mentality.

Her upbringing.

Her etiquette.

Even her namesake.

She was named *Noha.*

Brain.

In her time, a woman in Egypt was meant to be admired for her beauty, her kind manner.

My grandparents wanted *Mama* to be admired for her thinking.

Although she hated the limelight, *Mama* often found herself within it.

Her odd preference for pants rather than dresses or skirts.

The audacity to speak to a man, as well as look him in the eye.

Independent.

A scholar first and a wife second.

She was a popular talking point in her hometown.

She possessed the kind of beauty that ran scarce.

The unprecedented kind.

The unrivaled kind.

In a world that was dedicated to subduing a women's words, *Mama's* mouth burned bright.

~

My grandpa was called a fool for loving his daughter with the same ferocity as an Egyptian man loved his son.

When *Mama* left Egypt for France on scholarship to obtain her PhD with her husband and newborn child, it was those who were once in opposition who felt like the fools.

~

Like *Mama*, I was raised to be outspoken and deafening. To both strangers and loved ones alike, I was known as the girl who spoke her mind.

A man's mind in a woman's body, they said.

"No, better: a woman's mind in a woman's body," *Mama* often replied.

When family and neighbors scoffed at my manners, *Mama's* smile was heavy with praise.

~

When *Issam* died at the age of one year too young, *Mama* embraced the stereotypical expectations of both man and woman.

In her, my grandparents saw the son they lost.

When Ahmed came along shortly after, *Mama* had already grown accustomed to her appointed role, her adopted identity.

⌒

I was eleven when *Mama* told me about *Issam*.

As a young girl, the only Death I knew was the one scattered inside the bindings of my books and the movies my television harbored.

He had not punctured my reality, though he had caressed it. *Alhamdulelah*. Thank God.

Despite my ignorance, Death had been very aware of us. It wasn't until later that I recognized how close.

Issam appeared to have swallowed the sun.

Everything about him was bright.

His golden locks.

Bright green eyes.

He was my grandma's double.

People often stopped on the street to stare at him. He did not possess the typical Egyptian characteristics of black hair, dark eyes, sun-bleached skin like caramel.

It was said that he controlled the sun. It fed him. Indulged him.

My grandpa said Egypt had experienced its driest and warmest summer the year *Issam* descended on our terrain.

In the end, it was the sun that led to his downfall.

He contracted a diarrheal disease.

But it was the dehydration that killed him.

My mother was two years too young.

Too young to understand.

Old enough to sympathize. Old enough to recognize the dimness in exchange for the sunlight.

My grandparents say he had gathered too much attention. Had been too perfect.

A taunt to Death's name.

And Death always has the last word.

⟿

It stormed on the day *Issam* died.
Even the sun was mourning.

When the sun emerged from the clouds the following afternoon, it burned with a tenacious luster.

What had been taken was now returned.

In the brilliance, my grandparents' tears shone red.

⟿

"Do you miss him?"
"I don't remember him."

⟿

I had just turned ten when the same sickness that took *Issam* befell me. Twenty-five years later.

The summer of 2008. My family and I were visiting Egypt for the first time with my brother.

We were used to falling ill with each visit, but nothing to that degree.

In ten days, I had forfeited seventeen pounds.

My grandma could not bear to witness my suffering.

To her, she was losing *Issam* for the second time.

I was afforded the advances in medication.

Nine extra years to my name.

And a chubby body.

What *Issam* lacked, I possessed in excess.

I faced a different fate.

Mama says that it was my figure that led to my salvation.

Sugar was on my side, just this once.

My age outweighed Death's restless vicinity. My weight and medication triggered His dismissal.

⸮

I didn't understand how tomorrow could appear for some while others still lived in yesterday.

It surprised me how deep-rooted Pain could nest.

Pain wore as many masks as there were phases of the moon. While I recognized some, I was a stranger to the others.

Mama said she hoped I would stay this way.
Untouched.

She assured me that Pain possessed one foe:
Time.

"The greatest blessing *Allah* has given us is our ability to forget.
With time, old wounds heal, allowing new ones to flourish."

ـﺝ

In Islam, when a family loses a child, the child is said to escort
them to *Jenna*, paradise.
Their admission to an afterlife lacking the suffering below.

One of the few to witness *Allah* and all His glory.

ـﺝ

In Arabic, *Issam* possesses several connotations.

Safeguard.
Protector.
Saint.

Many years later, when I asked my grandma if she had known
the meaning, she said she had not.
At the time, she had simply liked the name.
Unknowingly, my grandparents had deduced *Issam's* fate.

His fate became a testament to his name.

~ɔ

I wish I had been aware of *Issam's* lingering presence in *Mama's* thoughts.

He had a possessive hold on her even then.

The two of them were bound: *Issam* became the spine to *Mama's* pages. She was tethered by his pull. Unable to tell a story that did not contain him.

I knew I had lost *Mama* when she started mentioning *Issam's* name in her sleep.

A subversive taunt to Life's endowment.

She was no longer able to distinguish between reality and fantasy. She had faded gradually and brought gloom where *Issam* had brought light. They became paradoxical in nature and analogous in circumstance.

The tumor had planted itself strategically in *Mama's* most renowned possession: her brain.

And it flowered, the roots of the cancer forsaking her life to make room for its own.

While *Issam's* namesake became his fate, *Mama's* became her demise.

~ɔ

When a parent dies in Islam, their unsettled dues may be repaid by their offspring.

Just as our relation is not severed in Death, our duties to our family remain as well.

Salvation is not just dependent on the individual's actions but may also be influenced by the teachings ingrained in their children.

We, the children, become a reflection of those who bore us.

ـے

When Death came for *Mama*, I found no roles to adopt that were not already appointed to me.

It was then that I recognized she had bequeathed me an identity that spared no expectations. One that did not include distinct gender roles or functions. Rather, she had snared all semblance of her assigned character and unearthed a daughter who had the rarity of choice.

To possess it all. Or part of it. To not be limited by the external expectations, only the internal.

In that way, I became a manifestation of her.
In my freedom of choice, she lives on.

And where she endures, *Issam* persists as well.

ـے

Where I come from, names are powerful.
Endued with meaning.

Indicative of an unfulfilled promise. A vision. A gift.
I believe we all find ways of embodying our name. Of making it our own.

Even my own.

Originally, it was decided that I would be named *Reem*. A white gazelle. Commonly associated with beauty and grace.

But after the arduous labor, *Mama* changed her mind. She would grant me something greater than elegance and attraction.

Identity.

I was named *Rana*. Eye-catching. To gaze at admiringly.

A name worthy for the daughter of an unconventional scholar.

A name whose receiver is not afraid to be seen, despite society's will to conceal her.
One who will push away from the wall and walk in the center.

البوابة إلى بارادايس

RANA HEWEZI

ترجمة إلى اللغة العربية بواسطة هند سعيد

كنْ كشروق الشمس، تمسك بالضوء حتى يلقي الظلام.

يقال إن الدموع هي حزنُ على الكلمات ،أن تظل رهينة للعقل.
خطوة رحيمة تسمح لنا بسماع ما تبقى مما لم يقال.

في اللغة الإنجليزية، tear لها معانٍ كثيرة.
أول ما يتبادر إلى ذهني ، إنها رواسب مالحة تذرفها العيون.
لكني دائمًا أفكر ومما يثير انتباهي، أنها تستعمل أيضاً ،لوصف شيئا ما قد مُزق
أو قُطعَ.
مُكوّنة شيئا لم يعد متكاملا.
ما عدا كونها تلفظ {ter} بدلا من {tir}.

كانوا متطابقتين في نظري.

في اللغة العربية، tears تلفظ {دمعة}.
أنها تشبه كلمة دم.

~

أكثر الناس لا يعلمون أن ماما ،كان لديها ثلاث أخوة.
أحدهم نجا من قبضة الحياة المنزلقة وبأنهُ قد قايضها بدلاً بقبضة الموت الثابتة.
أخ، لطالما عُلِّق أسمه على أطراف لسان ماما وأعمق أفكارها.
ألم ، لم تختار أن تنساه ، ولكنها لم تستطع أن تتذكره.

114

هو، بجانب الموت، أصابوا أفكارها.

عصام.

أسم، يذكرنا بأن الضعف والإنسانية متلاصقان مثل الكتاب وفقارته.
بينما تكون فقارة الكتاب هي مرتكز الكتاب، تكون أيضا معيقاً لمرونته.

مع ذلك، لا يمكننا أن نكون صفحات حرة. من لحظة ولادتنا، نحن مرتبطين بموت.
موعودين له من وقت تصورنا في الأرحام ونلتقيه عندما نتخلى عن نفس الحياة الحلو.
والموت لم يكن رحيما، لأن الذي يأخذ فقط لا يعرف أن يُعطي.

~

مثل بابا، ماما بإمكانها أن تشعر بالرابط القوي ما بين الخسارة والموت.
بينما نشأ بابا تحت الأضواء ، فضلت ماما أن تحتمي بالظل.
كبرت متحفظة وخائفة من عيون الموت الغامضة.
حذرة وبريئة.

جلبُ الأنظار اليها يعني الإفراط في الحياة التي اختلست من قبضة الموت التي لا تغفر.
يمكن لحديث المجتمع أن يُهمس بسهولة في أذان الموت.

هناك مقولة معروفة في اللغة العربية. نصيحة للهروب من مراقبة الناس والتي تقول أمشي
جنب الحيطة: {أمشي بجانب الحائط.}

بالرغم من أنه كان هناك طبيعة تشجيع على أن تكون المرأة تابعةً للرجل، لكن طبيعة
حياة ماما كانت ضد هذا التفكير
نشأتها.
آداب الحياة التي تعلمتها.

115

حتى أسمها الذي سّميت به.

~

كانت قد سُميت نُهى.
عقل.
في زمنها، كانت المرأة في مصر تُقدر لجمالها وأخلاقها الحسنة .
جدي وجَدتي، أرادوا لها أن تُحترم لتفكيرها.

~

بالرغم من أنها كرهت أن تكون تحت أنظار الناس . لكن لطالما ماما وجدت نفسها في الأضواء.
اختيارها الغير متعارف عليه ، للبس البنطال بدا من التنانير أو الفساتين.
جرأتها في التحدث مع رجل ، والنظر في عينيه أيضاً.
استقلاليتها.
عالمة أولاً ثم زوجة ثانياً.

كانت محور الحديث في مدينتها.

تملك ذلك النوع من الجمال المخيف.
لم يسبق أن رأى مثله أحد.
نوع لا شبيه له.
في عام، نذر نفسه لقمع كلمات المرأة ، أشتعل فم ماما لمعانا.

~

نعت جدي بالغباء لكونه أحب أبنته بنفس القوة حب الرجل المصري لأبنه.

لكن عندما سافرت ماما إلى فرنسا بعد حصولها على المنحة الدراسية للحصول على شهادة

الدكتوراة مع زوجها و طفلها الحديث الولادة، شعر حينها الذين عارضوها ،بالغباء.

~

مثل ماما ، تربيت على أن أكون صريحة وواثقة في كلامي مع الغرباء والاشخاص الذين أحبهم على السواء.لقد عُرفت بالبنت التي تتحدث بصراحة.

قالوا: عقل رجل في جسد امرأة.

"لا، الأفضل: عقل امرأة في جسد امرأة" تجيب ماما في معظم الأحيان.

عندما تسخر العائلة والجيران من تصرفاتي، تضع ماما أبتسامة ثقيلة بكبرياء.

~

عندما توفي عصام في عمر السنة ،صغيرا جداً، أتخذت ماما السلوك المتوقع لها من قبل الرجال والنساء.
فيها، وجد جدي وجدتي الابن الذي فقدوه.

عندما ولد أحمد بعد فترة قصيرة. كانت ماما قد اعتادت على دورها المنوط بها : هويتها المتبناة.

~

كنت في الحادية عشر من عمري، عندما أخبرتني ماما عن عصام.
كُنت صغيرة ، لم أكن أعرف عن الموت غير ذلك الموت المنتشر في ردفات كتبي والأفلام التي يعرضها التلفاز.

لم يخترق الموت واقعي، بالرغم من أنه عانقه بلطف.
الحمد لله.

117

بالرغم من جهلي له ، لكن الموت كان على علم بنا. اكتشفت كم هو قريبا لاحقا.

يبدو أن عصام قد ابتلع الشمس.

كل شيء عنه كان مضيئاً.

خصلات شعره الذهبية.

عيونه الخضراء اللامعة.

كان النسخة الثانية من جدتي.

يتوقف الناس في بعض الأحيان في الطريق لينظروا إليه. لم يكن يحمل الملامح المصرية التقليدية ،من الشعر الأسود والعيون السوداء والبشرة المحروقة من الشمس بلون الكراميل.

يقال أنه كان يتحكم بالشمس. تغذيهِ. تعتني به.

قال جدي أن مصر مَرت في أحر وأدفأ صيف في السنة التي جاء فيها عصام إلى أرضنا.

في النهاية، كانت الشمس هي سبب تدهوره.

أصيب بمرض الإسهال.

لكن الجفاف هو الذي قتله.

والدتي كانت في الثانية من عمرها، صغيرة جداً.

صغيرة على أن تفهم.

لكنها كبيرة لحد أنها تتعاطف. كبيرة لتشعر بالعتمة التي تبادلت مع ضوء الشمس.

قال جدي وجدتي ، أنه جذب الكثير من الأنتباه. كان متكاملا.

سخرية باسم الموت.

والموت دائما له الكلمة الأخيرة.

118

هبت عاصفة في اليوم الذي توفي فيه عصام.

حتى الشمس كانت في حالة حداد.

عندما ظهرت الشمس من بين الغيوم ، في المساء التالي، ظهر بريقها محترقا لامعا.

ما كان مأخوذا ، قد أُسترجع الآن.

في تلك الاشراقة ، ظهرت دموع جدي وجدتي حمراء.

~

"هل تشتاق إليه؟".

"أنا لا أتذكره؟.

~

قدموا لي العلاجات المتطورة.

تسعة سنوات أخرى أضيفت إلى عمري.

وجسد ممتلئ.

عندما كنت في العاشرة ، انتابني نفس مرض عصام. بعد خمس وعشرين سنة ، في صيف ٨٠٠٢. كنا أنا وعائلتي نزور مصر لأول مرة مع أخي.

أعتدنا أن نمرض في كل زيارة ، لكن ليس بهذه الدرجة.

خسرتُ سبعة عشر باوند في عشرة أيام.

لم تقوى جدتي على رؤية آلامي.

بالنسبة لها، أنها تخسر عصام للمرة الثانية.

119

ما لم يحصل عليه عصام ، كان عندي فائضا.

واجهت مصيراً آخر.

تقول ماما أن قوامي أدى الى خلاصي.

السكر يعمل لصالحي،هذه المرة فقط.

عمري تعدى حدود الموت المُضطربة. وزني وعلاجي ساعدا على فصله.

~

لم أفهم كيف أن الغد قد أتى للبعض بينما ما يزال الآخرون يعيشون في الأمس.

تفاجئت كيف يمكن لجذور الألم العميقة أن تعشش.

يلبس الألم أقنعة متعددة مثل مراحل عمر القمر. على الرغم من معرفتي ببعضها ،لكني لم
أكن أعرف الأخريات .

قالت ماما، أنها تتمنى أن أبقى كذلك.

على طبيعتي. لا أعرف.

أكدت لي أن الالم يَتملكُ عدو الإنسان : الوقت.

أن أفضل ما منحه الله لنا هو قدرتنا على النسيان.

مع الوقت، الجروح القديمة تندمل وتسمح للجروح الجديدة بالنمو.

~

في الإسلام، يقال إنه عندما تفقد العائلة طفلا ،فإنه يأخذهم الى الجنة، esidarap.

رسمُ لدخولهم الآخرة، يجنبهم المعاناة في جهنم.

القلة التي تشهد لله وعظمته.

~

في اللغة العربية، أسم عصام يحمل الكثير من الدلالات والمعاني.

120

الحامي.

المدافع.

القديس.

~

بعد سنين طويلة ، سألت جدتي فيما إذا كانت تعرف هذه المعاني ، قالت أنها لم تعرفها في
ذلك الحين . انها اسمته لأنها ببساطة أحبت الاسم.
ومن دون أن يعلموا ، جدي وجدتي استنبطوا مصير عصام.
مصيره كان دليلا على أسمه.

~

كنت أتمنى لو أني شعرت بحضور عصام الدائم في أفكار ماما.
كان له طريقة بتملك أفكارها حتى في ذلك الحين.
كانوا الأثنين مترابطين: أصبح عصام العمود الفقري لصفحات ماما. كانت مقيدة بسحبه لها.
غير قادرة على أن تحكي قصة من دون أن يكون ضمنها.

علمت أني خسرت ماما عندما بدأت تذكر أسمه في نومها.
سخرية سوداء لهبة الحياة.

لم تعد قادرة على أن تفرق بين الحقيقة والخيال.بدأت تذبل تدريجيا وجلبت عتمة بينما
كان عصام قد جلب ضوءاً. أصبحوا متناقضين في طبيعتهم و متشابهين في ظروفهم.

زرع الورم نفسه بإستراتيجية في أفضل ما تملكه ماما: عقلها .
وانتعش وتورد وامتدت جذور السرطان لتفسح المجال لنفسها وتخلت عن ماما.
بينما أصبحت تسمية عصام هي مصيره ، اصبح اسم ماما نهايتها.

~

121

عندما يموت الوالدين في الإسلام ، يقوم الأولاد بدفع المستحقات المترتبة عليهم.
كما أن علاقاتنا لا تنتهي بالموت ، واجباتنا تجاه عائلتنا تبقى هي أيضاً.
الخلاص لا يعتمد على الأفعال الشخصية لكن يمكن أن يتأثر أيضا بالتعليمات التي غرزت
في أولادهم.
نحن، الأولاد، نصبح انعكاسا لمن أنجبونا للحياة.

~

عندما أتى الموت لماما، لم أجد لي أي دور غير الدور الذي مقرر لي.

حينها تنبهت أنها أورثتني شخصية فائقة التوقعات .لا تلتزم بدور أو عمل خاص بجنس
ما . بل، أنها أخذت ما يمثل شخصيتها لتكشف عن أبنة لديها اختيارات نادرة.
للحصول على كل شيء ، أو جزء منه . أن لا تكون متحددة في التوقعات الخارجية ،بل فقط
بالتوقعات الداخلية.

وبهذه الطريقة، أصبحتُ ما يمثلها.
في حريتي في الاختيار، تعيش هي.
وعندما تتحمل وتصمد، عصام يستمر أيضاً.

~

من المكان الذي أتيت منه ،الأسماء لها قوة.
مليئة بالمعاني.

مؤشر بصورة غير مباشرة الى وعود لم تتحقق. رؤية. هدية.
أعتقد أن كل منا يجد طرقا لتجسيد أسمائنا ، وجعلها ملكنا.

حتى أسمي.

~

في البداية ، كان من المقرر أن أسمى ريم . غزال أبيض. اسم مرتبط بالجمال والنعمة. لكن بعد معاناة الولادة الشاقة، غيرت ماما تفكيرها. ومنحتني شيئا أعظم من الانجذاب والأناقة.

هوية.

سُميت رنا .أسم يجذب الأنظار. للتحديق به بإعجاب. أسم يليق بأبنة الباحثة الغير تقليدية.

أسم، حاملته لا تخاف من أن تُرى بالرغم من أن المجتمع يود أن يتحفظ عليها. تدفع نفسها بعيدا عن الحائط لتسير إلى وسط.

ANTHONY MIELKE

ARTIST STATEMENT

I WAS BORN to a Puerto Rican father and Minnesotan mother but was raised far away from my father and his family. For most of my life, my Puerto Rican identity was denied and repressed. I lived so long with a gnawing sense that there was something more to my story than I was living or was allowed to live. But until recently, I didn't have language to describe this experience or a way to understand it. Through writing, I have come to understand my story and have found the language to share it.

Writing has guided me into my own story and given me the courage and compassion to embrace and share it. It was my companion and anchor as the pillars of my world crumbled and new ones were built in their place. It came to me at a crucial point in my life and, in a very real way, it saved my life in the midst of unthinkable upheaval. It is a quiet, sacred space where I continue to learn the language of my inner landscapes and ease myself into my rapidly evolving world.

I continue to struggle with how to define myself. When I went to write my story, I wanted to say, "This is me. This is where I was, this is where I am, and this is where I think I am going." Then I realized I was writing in the same way I had lived for a very long time: I was trying to tell my story in such a way that whoever read it couldn't possibly not believe me. I was writing in the shape of a shield big enough to hide behind if anyone tried to get too close.

This is how I lived for most of my life. I always felt out of place, like an imposter who was one misstep away from being exposed and discarded. I built walls and shields and arrows around me in order to hide my secret, all the while not even knowing what secret I was guarding. In my early pages of opaque, intellectual run-on sentences, I found that wall again and, behind it, the part of me that was always scared once my secret was out. I took down the shield and wrote this essay.

For the first time in my life, I know the breadth and width of my story and am not afraid of it. I can celebrate my story now, and I am grateful for the opportunity to share it.

STRANGER IN MY OWN WORLD

ANTHONY MIELKE

AS A YOUNG CHILD, I found a picture of my dad and me shortly after I was born. In it, he is sitting on my grandparents' couch, holding me, cradling my head in his hand and leaning over, his face close to mine. I loved looking at that picture and was always intrigued by the man holding me, whom I only knew as Orlando. At some point in my childhood, that picture disappeared. And until 2016, this was the only time I saw or touched my father.

In 2009, when I was twenty, he found me online while I was studying abroad in Rome. After years of failed attempts to contact me through my mom, he decided it was time to reach out to me directly and sent me a brief message through Facebook. He wished me a happy early and very belated birthday and said I would recognize him by his picture. He was right. Even before I read the message, I knew my dad had found me. On the screen was a stranger with my face and eyes and hair, staring back at me like a legend come to life. Until that moment, I never realized it was the first time I saw a face that looked like mine. As I looked at his Facebook profile, I was reminded of the many nights I would stand in front of my bedroom mirror, staring at my eyes, cheekbones, and lips, wishing they didn't look they way they looked but never knowing what exactly was wrong with them. I found the answer that day in my dad's face: the reason I thought I looked "wrong" all those years was because I am Puerto Rican, like him.

Years after the first message in 2009, I learned that my dad tried to visit for my birthdays, offer money to help my mom, and send letters to me throughout my childhood. I also learned that my Great-Grandma Isabel, known simply as *Abuela*, wrote my mom letters in Spanish before I was born and during my early years. My mom never had them translated, though, and didn't tell me about

129

them until 2016. When I learned this, I was devastated. Even before I was born, my story was silenced and left to fade away. I ache to read those words from *Abuela*, to see her heart and hear her speak to me from the past. But my mom lost the letters, so I never will.

Growing up, my origin story was told to me in fragments. My mom is Caucasian and was born and raised in rural Minnesota. My dad is Puerto Rican and grew up in both Puerto Rico and the South Bronx. They met while working at a summer camp in upstate New York, and after trying to make a life together, they separated. My mom moved back to Minnesota with her parents, and my father stayed in New York City.

I was raised by my mom and stepdad in rural Minnesota. My mom and stepdad are devout Catholics and political and social conservatives. In my mom's eyes, being a single mother of a Latino child was shameful, and the suppression of this reality gave rise to a new, false narrative about my beginnings. My mom occasionally reminded me that she lost a teaching job at a Catholic school after becoming pregnant and was ostracized from our local church until she and my stepdad married. She told me I was not given my dad's last name in order to protect me from the racist attitudes toward Latinos in our small community. I also found out they had a small, private wedding in order to avoid the appearance of scandal in the church, since I was already five years old and not my stepdad's biological son.

As a child, I had no conscious awareness of being raised in a blended family as an adopted Puerto Rican. My early years were seen as a story of heroic redemption undertaken by my mom and stepdad. According to the family lore, my stepdad selflessly assumed financial responsibility for us, saved me from growing up fatherless, and gave us a life unimaginably better than the one we would have had without him. While I felt supported and cared for by my stepdad, I know now that this narrative was fed by a culture of lies perpetuated to erase the sins of the past. The story I embodied could not be forgotten, so it was demonized and suppressed.

My mom and stepdad carefully coached me how to respond when I was asked about my difference. If asked why I was the only person in my family with brown eyes, I explained that someone had brown eyes in my mom's family, even though I never knew who it was. When friends asked about my dark complexion in the summer, I explained how tan my mom would get as a teenage lifeguard at the community pool. Over and over I explained away my difference, always desperately hoping that my deflections would be enough to avoid more questions. I held a private shame and knew my story needed to stay silenced. It felt like loyalty to lie for the sake of my family's integrity. These deflections usually worked, and the secret stayed hidden.

As I grew older, I internalized the shame and fear that surrounded my story. This shame buried my identity so deep that when my Latino coworkers at a summer job in high school came to me one day and exclaimed, "You're one of us!", I was so taken aback and confused that they had to repeat themselves over and over. Each time they said it, I grew more afraid and more frantic. I lied right to their faces, believing I could erase and rewrite reality, just like my parents did to me. Looking back, I don't think I could admit to being Latino that day because it would have meant acknowledging that my family had not just rejected and buried my mom's story but that they had also done the same to mine.

When my dad contacted me on Facebook, I could not consciously accept that there was more to my story than I was living. I could not accept that I was lied to and had internalized that lie so completely that I clung to the censored narrative of my life as if there were pride and honor in the shame. I could not consider the possibility of loving this man who left me before I was born but had loved me from a distance my whole life. I didn't want to know why he left. I didn't want anything to do with him or whatever truth he held. In my mind, I was a successful, respectful, and strong young white man, destined for great things and unencumbered by my disjointed, complicated beginnings.

I didn't write back to my dad for four years, although he continued to send cordial messages on my birthday and holidays. To me, speaking with him represented a betrayal of the parents who raised me, especially my stepdad. But when my wife and I were expecting our first baby, I felt it was time to give our relationship a chance, especially now that I was about to be a father and did not want to raise my daughter in a culture of shame and secrets. So, I sent him a formal message explaining my education, work, and family life. I wanted him to know that I didn't need him growing up and didn't need him now. He replied almost immediately and we began a few years of occasional written exchanges.

In the summer of 2016, I decided I was ready to meet my dad in person and invited him to Minnesota. We agreed to meet at a Minneapolis cafe on the first day. As I drank cup after cup of coffee, I could only stare at the door and trust that whatever was about to happen would be for the good. I sat in shock as he entered the cafe and approached my table. The whole brunch, we talked at a feverish pace and kept touching each other's arms and hands just to remember it was really happening. By the end of his four-day visit, I was becoming alive to myself in ways I never thought possible. So much of him lived inside me but had been suppressed and silenced by years of shame. His vibrant energy, his passion and sense of wonder, his belief in the goodness of others, and his intense love all lived in me and were finally given space to breathe in his company.

Later that year, I went to New York City to meet the rest of my Puerto Rican family. Before this trip, I never would have imagined that they would remember me or wait for me all these years. I thought I was long forgotten. But the first night I met my grandmother, Margarita, she touched my cheek like it was something she had done for decades, like she had held me all those years. And in that touch, I knew the family was waiting for me the whole time and holding space for me until I came home. That trip was filled with intense celebration, deep sadness, and real hope for a life together moving forward.

While my mom and stepdad initially seemed supportive of my emerging identity, I came to realize that the suppression of my origin story was only one part of a larger pattern of suppression in my family. Coming into my Puerto Rican identity was a vital step in moving away from that environment and into a more authentic version of myself. At this point in time, my mom and stepdad still have not accepted responsibility for or acknowledged the destructive effects of their efforts to be free from the past.

Since those first meetings, I have slowly become aware of how my father's absence and my family's silence shaped and colored my world. As the silence lifted and secrets were aired, my story began to unfold in new, profound, and painful ways. I finally understood why my deflections were so important to my family's script: by merely existing, I posed a threat to the safety of this dark family secret. I look like my dad, talk like him, laugh like him, think like him, sing like him, play like him, and dream like him. But I was never told these things growing up and felt constant embarrassment and self-doubt. I only knew that I lived under a microscope and carried the weight of my mom's redemption and stepdad's heroism on my shoulders. My whitewashing and sterilization were constant proof that their past was indeed dead.

I am only now gradually acquiring the language to describe a lifelong sense of being a stranger in my own world. I felt isolated from others and myself, like I couldn't quite touch or be touched. I always thought it was my fault, and it was up to me to fix it. I thought it was my burden to carry. Before meeting my dad, I didn't even know how to say where it hurt, let alone how to heal whatever it was that was hurting.

Now, I don't feel alone. My father and the rest of my Puerto Rican family have accepted me unconditionally. They have supported me as I struggle with my past and integrate my emerging self with my old way of being in the world. With their support and love, I am no longer ashamed of being Puerto Rican. I am proud of my identity and my ever-evolving story. I am no longer a stranger in my own world.

UN EXTRAÑO EN MI PROPIO MUNDO

ANTHONY MIELKE
TRADUCCIÓN AL ESPAÑOL POR NIEVES MARTÍN LÓPEZ

DE PEQUEÑO, encontré una fotografía de mi padre y yo, poco después de mi nacimiento. En la fotografía, él aparece sentado en el sofá de mis abuelos, sujetándome y acunando mi cabeza entre sus manos, reclinado con su cara junto a la mía. Yo amaba mirar esa imagen y siempre me intrigaba ese hombre que me sujetaba, al que yo solo conocía como Orlando. En algún momento de mi infancia, esa fotografía desapareció. Hasta 2016, ese breve instante fue la única vez en que vi o toqué a mi padre.

En 2009, cuando yo tenía 20 años y estaba estudiando en Roma, él me encontró por internet. Tras años intentando contactarme sin éxito a través de mi madre, decidió que era hora de ponerse en contacto conmigo directamente y me envió un breve mensaje por Facebook. Me deseó feliz cumpleaños –por adelantado y también por los de años atrás– y me dijo que lo reconocería por su foto. Tenía razón. Incluso antes de leer el mensaje, ya sabía que mi padre me había encontrado. En la pantalla había un extraño con mi misma cara y mi pelo, mirándome fijamente como el personaje de una leyenda, ahora en carne y hueso. Hasta aquel momento nunca había visto una cara que se pareciera a la mía. Y mientras miraba su perfil de Facebook, recordé todas las noches que me había parado frente al espejo de mi habitación, contemplando mis ojos, pómulos, labios, deseando que no tuvieran la forma que tienen, pero sin saber exactamente qué tenían de malo. Ese día encontré la respuesta en la cara de mi padre. Todo lo que veía de malo en mí mismo durante esos años era que soy puertorriqueño, como él.

Años después de aquel mensaje en 2009, descubrí que durante toda mi niñez, mi padre había tratado de visitarme en mis cumpleaños, ofrecer dinero para ayudar a mi madre y enviarme cartas. También descubrí que mi bisabuela Isabel, a la que llamaban solo Abuela, le escribió cartas en español a mi madre antes de mi nacimiento y durante mis primeros años. Sin embargo, mi madre nunca quiso que se las tradujeran, y hasta 2016, nunca me las mencionó. Cuando me enteré de todo esto, me quedé destrozado. Incluso antes de nacer, mi historia había sido silenciada y condenada a desaparecer. Deseaba con toda mi alma leer esas palabras de Abuela, ver su corazón y escucharla hablarme desde el pasado. Pero mi madre perdió las cartas, así que ya nunca podré.

De chico, la historia de mis orígenes se me contó en fragmentos. Mi madre es blanca, caucásica; nació y creció en la Minnesota rural. Mi padre es puertorriqueño y creció entre Puerto Rico y el sur del Bronx. Se conocieron cuando trabajaban en un campamento de verano en el norte del estado de Nueva York, y tras intentar componer una vida juntos, se separaron. Mi madre volvió a Minnesota con sus padres, mientras que mi padre se quedó en la ciudad de Nueva York.

Mi madre y mi padrastro me criaron en la zona rural de Minnesota. Ambos son católicos devotos y conservadores, en lo político y lo social. A ojos de mi madre, ser madre soltera de un hijo latino era algo deshonroso, y la represión de esa realidad generó una nueva narrativa falsa sobre mis orígenes. En ocasiones mi madre me recordaba que había perdido un trabajo de profesora en una escuela católica luego de haberse quedado embarazada, y que la dejaron fuera de nuestra iglesia local hasta que ella y mi padrastro estuvieran casados. Me contó que no me había puesto el apellido de mi padre para protegerme del racismo hacia los latinos dentro de nuestra pequeña comunidad rural. También averigüé que ellos tuvieron una boda privada y muy pequeña para evitar un escándalo en la iglesia, porque yo ya tenía cinco años y no era el hijo biológico de mi padrastro.

De niño, yo no era consciente de haber crecido en una familia como niño puertorriqueño-americano adoptado. Mis primeros años se consideraban la historia de la heroica redención que sufrieron mi madre y mi padrastro. Según esa historia, mi padrastro se hizo cargo de nosotros económicamente de manera desinteresada, me salvó de crecer sin padre, y nos dio una vida indudablemente mejor que la que habríamos tenido sin él. A la vez que me sentí apoyado y bien

135

cuidado por mi padrastro, sé que esta narrativa se alimentó de un cultivo de mentiras perpetuadas para borrar los pecados del pasado. Yo era la encarnación de una historia que no podía ser olvidada, así que era demonizada y reprimida.

Mi madre y mi padrastro me adiestraron con detalle en las respuestas que debía dar cuando me preguntaran por mi aspecto diferente. Si me preguntaban por qué era el único de mi familia con ojos marrones, les explicaba que venían por parte de un familiar de mi madre, pero que nunca supe quién fue. Cuando mis amigos me preguntaban por mi piel oscura durante el verano, les explicaba lo morena que se ponía mi madre cuando de joven trabajaba como socorrista en la piscina comunitaria. Justificaba mis diferencias una y otra vez, siempre tratando de que mis evasivas bastaran para frenar más preguntas. Me sentía humillado por dentro y sabía que mi historia debía seguir silenciada; me mantenía fiel a la mentira para proteger la integridad de la familia. Normalmente, mis evasivas funcionaban, y el secreto seguía siendo secreto.

Al hacerme mayor, internalicé esa vergüenza y ese miedo que rodeaban mi historia. La vergüenza consiguió enterrar mi identidad tan profundamente que cuando mis colegas latinos de un trabajo de verano llegaron un día y me dijeron: "¡Oye, tú eres uno de nosotros!", me tomó tan desprevenido y me dejó tan confuso que me lo tuvieron que repetir varias veces. Cada vez que lo repetían, yo me volvía más asustado y ansioso. Les mentí a la cara, pensando que podía borrar y reescribir la realidad, tal como habían hecho mis padres conmigo. Mirando hacia atrás, en ese momento no creo que hubiera podido admitir que soy latino, porque habría supuesto reconocer que mi familia no solo había rechazado y enterrado la historia de mi madre, sino también la mía.

Cuando mi padre me contactó por Facebook, no podía aceptar que mi historia era algo más que lo que era mi vida hasta entonces. No podía aceptar que me hubieran mentido y que yo hubiera internalizado esa mentira ciegamente, llegando a aferrarme a esa narrativa censurada de mi vida como si mi honor y orgullo se alimentaran de la vergüenza. No podía considerar la posibilidad de querer a ese hombre que me dejó antes de nacer, pero que me había querido desde la distancia durante toda mi vida. Yo no quería saber por qué se fue. No quería tener nada que ver con él o con cualquiera que fuera esa verdad que él representara. En mi mente, yo era un joven blanco, fuerte, exitoso y respetable, destinado a grandes cosas y libre de las cargas de mis inicios complicados e inconexos.

Pasé cuatro años sin contestarle, aunque él siguió enviándome mensajes cordiales en mi cumpleaños y en los festivos. Para mí, hablar con él representaba traicionar a los padres que me criaron, especialmente mi padrastro. Pero cuando mi mujer y yo esperábamos nuestra primera hija, sentí que era hora de darle una oportunidad a mi padre biológico. Ahora que yo iba a ser padre, no quería criar a mi niña en una cultura de humillación y secretos, como la que tuve yo. Así pues, le envié un mensaje formal a mi padre hablándole sobre mi educación, mi trabajo y mi vida familiar. Quería que supiera que no lo necesité para criarme y que no lo necesitaba ahora. Me respondió casi de inmediato, y así empezamos a escribirnos ocasionalmente durante un par de años.

En el verano de 2016, decidí que estaba preparado para conocer a mi padre en persona, así que lo invité a Minnesota. El primer día acordamos encontrarnos en una cafetería de Minneapolis. Mientras tomaba un café tras otro, no paraba de mirar la puerta de la cafetería y confiar en que, fuera lo que fuera que iba a pasar, sería algo bueno. Me quedé paralizado cuando entró en la cafetería y se acercó a mi mesa. Durante toda la comida, hablamos sin cesar y no paramos de tocar las manos y los brazos del otro, para recordarnos que aquello estaba sucediendo de verdad. Después de su visita de cuatro días, yo comencé a sentirme vivo de una forma que nunca pensé que fuera posible. Había tanto de él dentro de mí, pero los años de deshonra y represión lo habían acallado hasta ese momento. Su personalidad energética y apasionada, esa ilusión, su firme creencia en la bondad de los demás y todo ese intenso amor vivían en mi interior, y por fin podían salir a flote y respirar cuando estaba a su lado.

Unos meses después ese mismo año fui a Nueva York a conocer al resto de mi familia puertorriqueña. Antes del viaje, nunca me habría imaginado que ellos me recordarían o que me hubieran esperado después de tantos años. Pensé que me habrían olvidado muchos años atrás, pero la noche en que conocí a mi abuela Margarita, me acarició la mejilla como si lo hubiera hecho durante décadas, como si me hubiera abrazado desde siempre. Y en esa caricia descubrí que la familia me había estado esperando todo ese tiempo y que me habían reservado un hueco entre ellos hasta que volviera a mi hogar. Ese viaje estuvo lleno de intensas celebraciones, una profunda tristeza y verdadera esperanza por una vida en común a partir de ese momento.

Mientras que mi madre y mi padrastro en un principio parecían apoyarme con mi identidad incipiente, me di cuenta de que la represión de mis orígenes era solo una parte de un patrón mayor de represión y abusos en mi familia. El descubrir y aceptar mi identidad puertorriqueña fue un paso vital para alejarme de ese ambiente y convertirme en una versión más auténtica de mí mismo. Hasta el día de hoy, mi madre y mi padrastro todavía no han asumido la responsabilidad ni reconocido los efectos devastadores que tuvieron en mi vida sus esfuerzos por librarse del pasado.

Desde esos primeros encuentros con mi padre, me he dado cuenta poco a poco de la forma en que su ausencia y el silencio de mi familia han moldeado y coloreado mi mundo. Conforme el silencio desaparecía y se destapaban los secretos, mi historia comenzó a desvelarse de formas nuevas, profundas, dolorosas. Al fin comprendí por qué mis desviaciones eran tan importantes en el guion familiar. Solo por existir ya suponía una amenaza para ese oscuro secreto de familia. Yo me parezco a mi padre: hablo como él, me río como él, pienso como él, canto como él, juego como él y sueño como él. Pero nadie me dijo estas cosas durante mi infancia, y eso provocó en mí un sentimiento de constante vergüenza y baja autoestima. Solo sabía que vivía bajo un escrutinio incesante y que llevaba a cuestas el peso de la redención de mi madre y el heroísmo de mi padrastro. Al esterilizar y cubrir mi historia con una fachada blanca, ellos intentaban probar una y otra vez que su pasado estaba bien muerto y enterrado.

Ahora es cuando poco a poco empiezo a adquirir el lenguaje para describir toda una vida sintiéndome un extraño en mi propio mundo. Me sentía aislado de mí mismo y de otros, como si no pudiera realmente tocar o sentir el tacto de los demás. Siempre pensé que era mi culpa, que era algo que yo debía arreglar, que era una carga que solo yo debía llevar a cuestas. Antes de conocer a mi padre, ni siquiera sabía qué era lo que me dolía, mucho menos cómo curar esa herida.

Ya no me siento solo. Mi padre y el resto de mi familia puertorriqueña me han aceptado incondicionalmente. Me han apoyado en mi lucha interna con mi pasado y en la integración de mi nuevo yo con mi vieja historia de existencia. Con su apoyo y amor, ya no me avergüenzo de ser puertorriqueño. Estoy orgulloso de mi identidad y mi historia en constante desarrollo. Ya no soy un extraño en mi propio mundo.

DAWSON DAVENPORT

ARTIST STATEMENT

I WAS BORN a member of the Meskwaki Nation, located in Tama County, Iowa. I am a Meskwaki before anything. I am a recent graduate of the University of Iowa as well, majoring in art and getting a certificate in entrepreneurial management. I am also a convicted felon.

I create art to share about how life is as a Native person today. I share parts of myself and the things that have made me who I am up to this point in my life. This is my first time telling a lot of these stories. I've always told these in safe spaces, in therapy groups, in AA. I write these stories now for the public, with the hope of helping people, especially young Native people, who may be struggling in life. I hope I can uplift and inspire that Native kid who might feel like his life is worthless because he made a bad choice.

Even though I am afraid I might lose everything I've worked for in sharing these stories, it's worth it if means helping Native people better their way of living. I love my people. I want them to know that if you hit rock bottom, you can find your way up out of that and make things better for yourself.

I am a Meskwaki before anything. We tell stories. This is only the beginning of the story, because the story is still being written.

BLACK THUNDER:
A MESKWAKI STORY

BY DAWSON DAVENPORT
IN COLLABORATION WITH ANDREA WILSON

I AM THE MATERNAL GRANDSON of Abyekoneaka and Eskibakakea. Their white names are Curtis Davenport and Lois Waseskuk Davenport. I am Makatenenemekiwa. Translated, it means "Black Thunder." But you can call me Dawson.

I was given a Thunder Clan name by my great-grandfather Wabinenemekiwa. Meskwakis are born into a clan system based on our fathers. Clans are responsible for certain things within our tribe; to my understanding, Thunder Clan, or Wemiko, is responsible for peace and for interpreting on behalf of the tribe. I understand that the Thunder Clan is also responsible for taking care of everything associated with storms. A thunderstorm starts with overcast skies, and then that cold or warm front comes through. It brings with it the Thunder beings, very old spirits who come by to bless us and carry away the bad things with their high winds and heavy rains. At least, that's how they explained it to me when I was little.

I was raised by my maternal grandparents. My parents were kids when they made me, not ready to be parents, caught up in the trappings young Native people go through, like substance abuse. I don't know much about their relationship—they were young and messing around and then I came.

I was born in 1980 in Marshalltown, Iowa, but I don't know the story of my birth. I don't know if my mother rushed to the hospital, or who was with her, or what was she doing before she had me. Was she walking around home and started having contractions? I don't know, and no one ever told me about that day. I have only seen faded pictures of myself as a toddler wearing funky sunglasses at the kitchen table in the house where I grew up.

I was not close to my parents as a child. My mom came in and out of my life, and I didn't know who my father was until

143

I was fifteen. I had an idea of who he was from everyone telling me how much I resembled him, but he never made any attempt to acknowledge me. I don't know much about my dad's family, either. I have learned throughout the years about them, but I am not as close to them as I am to my mom's side of the family. When I was growing up, having absent parents seemed to become a new thing among Natives, the destruction of the family dynamic. Not only had we endured so much as a people, but with the world changing around us, we also had to adapt, getting jobs and a higher education. The pressures of society had spewed into my life and left me with a parentless childhood. Since I wasn't claimed by my father when I was born, my maternal grandfather and his father took me in as a member of the Thunder Clan.

Our last name, before we changed it to a white name, was Sakime, which means "mosquito." It was when white people came and the Census Bureau needed last names that we changed. Often our last names were misinterpreted, and that's how many of us got stuck with Americanized names, like Mauskemo, Pushetonqua, and Waseskuk. These names were spelled this way by census workers but are not actually Meskwaki text, because we do not have a written language. It was when linguists started coming around that we adopted a written language. As for us, the Davenports, how we got our white name is a special story. As I was told, Colonel Davenport, the man Davenport, Iowa, is named after, had daughters who married into our family. My great-great-grandfather decided to take his wife's white name instead of asking her to take his.

Our language is hard to interpret in English. It's a descriptive language, with no singular meaning. For example, we don't have a word for red. The word in Meskwaki for the color red is *meskwi* (pronounced *mesh-kwi*), the word for blood. If I wear a shirt that is red, we say the color is blood.

Meskwaki means "Red Earth People." The place where *meskwi* is held, the body, is believed to have come from the red clay we were created from. Eskibakakea, my grandma's name, means "green," as in green grass. Her name correlates with all that comes from a thunderstorm—new life, the blessings of the Thunder beings.

WHERE THE WEEPING WILLOWS SING

AN HOUR AND A HALF WEST of the University of Iowa lies a piece of land that is home to the Meskwaki Nation, who have been living in this area since the 1700s, well before the State of Iowa was founded in 1846 and the University of Iowa was founded in 1847. Those are my people, and the Meskwaki Settlement is my home.

I grew up on the Settlement, or the Sett, as we say for short, a beautiful land tucked away by the Iowa River, originally a small eighty acres that has grown and flourished since my ancestors made it our homeland all those years ago. A place where the fog rolls in and the weeping willows sing in the early summer mornings. A place where the squirrels bounce around the tops of trees like pinballs in a machine. A place where the oaks and the maples exchange pleasantries in their respective languages as the wind passes. This little piece of land located in Iowa, my ancestors prayed for with future generations in mind. A place where we could raise our children and plant our crops and practice our religion in peace.

This land has a beautiful history and a not-so-beautiful history, and living in that balance of the storm brews a narrative from the thunder that rumbles at night, the black thunder—Makatenenemekiwa.

For hundreds of years before the Settlement was officially established, the Meskwaki, or Red Earth People, federally known as the Sac and Fox of the Mississippi, lived in this region of the country. After being forcibly removed many times—by the French, the Americans, and other tribes—from our original homeland in the St. Lawrence River Valley of Ontario, the Meskwaki ended up in Iowa, where we lived for many years until again we were forced to move by the government and settlers. We moved west through Iowa, where we were told we were being sent to Oklahoma. Some Meskwaki began to walk south, but some stayed behind. Around 1847, when the government started drawing lines across the country and claiming ownership of the land as states, the Meskwaki who stayed behind worked out an agreement with a local farmer and the governor, and that is where we live now, on the Meskwaki Settlement in Tama County. We then sent people to go and tell those making the walk to Oklahoma to come back, that we had land for us and that it was okay. Some made it back, but others fell ill or were killed.

We were a people trying to survive great change from a foreign people taking over our way of life. Our Meskwaki way of life had worked for centuries. We knew how we were going to live from season to season—we were connected to our world and to the Earth. Some people think of tribes as always being in a group together, but we were spread out, based on a family's preference. Still, we were always connected. We had winter camps and summer camps. Our traditional housing changed with the seasons as well, from bark homes to cattail-mat homes.

The changes in our food system and environment were devastating, and the introduction of laws began to limit us in our way of life. Now, we were forced to live within boundaries. We could no longer go where we knew our medicines or other vital resources were due to the threat of being bothered not only by white people but also by their legal system. Now, going to cut wood or hunt outside our borders became a crime and could land us in jail. We had the education system and churches trying to teach us their ways. Our elders feared we would lose our traditions and our language. They feared we would assimilate and forget what a special people we are. We, a people used to being free, were now congested on eighty acres of land.

For the remainder of the nineteenth century, we were ignored and forgotten. We had to find our own ways to maintain our lives, where we turned to our arts and crafts and our crops to make money. We held good relations with our neighbors, and we stayed to ourselves, adapting to this ever-changing world around us while trying hard to keep our identity intact.

After the Indian Removal Act of 1830, the government began another round of assimilation tactics, removing Native children from their homes and sending them to boarding schools. A popular quote of the time by Captain Richard H. Pratt was "Kill the Indian, save the man." Indian Residential Schools had a history of sexual and psychological abuse. They beat the children for speaking their Native languages, and they cut off their hair, which was sacred.

This policy continued until about 1956 with the introduction of the Indian Relocation Act, a program designed to take us away from our communities under the guise of jobs and a better life in the big cities of America. After forcing us away into the schools, they decided to make us assimilate all the way. They decided to make us Americans.

As a child, I never learned about the tragedies that happened to my people. I didn't know about boarding school or about the Indian Relocation Act; I had to find out those things on my own, through books. I think it was simply too painful for my grandparents to talk about. But our tribe's history was different than many because we bought our land, which is why it is a settlement instead of a reservation. We were not immune to the hardships of reservation life; we still went through the same things, we just had a different outcome. In fact, because we were not on a reservation, we didn't qualify for some of the things the reservations got, and we were left to fend for ourselves. The Settlement was a place the American government put us so they could forget we existed. They just sent our monthly commods, as if boxes of processed meats, powdered eggs, instant milk, and blocks of cheese were their way of showing they cared.

We still live with the trauma of such policies, and we still deal with their effects. Natives are the only group members who have to carry a card to prove we are Native and belong to a tribe. There are active systems in place today, like blood quantum, that still try to dismantle us as Native people. We believe that if you have any of our blood in you, you are part of us, but the American government's blood quantum system says you must have a certain percentage to be recognized. This slowly kills the tribe, saying we don't exist. Our health is silently killing us, too. We have obesity issues and chronic health problems, partly from living off the foods in those death boxes.

When I read the history of what happened to our people in the white man's history books, I know some parts are true from the stories I've heard spoken by elders growing up, but they speak about them as if they just occurred, not long ago. My elders speak of our relatives who were alive at that time as if they are still around. In the

Western history books, the past is a two-dimensional list of dates and things that happened. For us, we talk about the past by saying who was there, because it's our story about our relatives. We know the true story of our past with the white man, what happened and why it happened the way it did. We know because our people were there and we pass these stories down through oral traditions. You probably wouldn't believe them if I told you. Much of our people's story didn't make the history books, and we aren't interested in contributing to that narrative anyway. We'd rather tell our story ourselves.

As Meskwakis, the way we talk about time in general is different. For us, there is only the past and the present. The future doesn't exist yet, so we don't talk about it. We can't speak on things that haven't happened yet. We look for signs in Nature to tell us when things begin and end. For us, human time operates with Nature's time—they are the same. Nature tells us when to do things like when to plant corn or harvest it. The winter tells us what kind of spring and summer we're going to have and the fall tells us what kind of winter is coming so we can prepare.

In our world, time and the things that happen all come to us through the Creator. Everything in our lives, we attribute to the Creator. Whatever happens, we believe that the Creator made it happen. And everything that happened, happened because we prayed.

We are taught that we are special people because of our connection to our Creator. We consider him our grandfather. That's how close we are to him—or her. (I don't put a gender on our Creator because we were made in the Creator's image, so that means we're all the same.)

As human beings, we don't know what the plan is. Only the Creator knows the plan. Difficult things have happened to our people. We believe that all of these things, even going to almost extinction, are part of a great plan.

There's a story our people tell about how we came to Iowa. It has to do with a bow and arrow. We lived with our Creator then, but change was about to come. The Creator shot an arrow from a great bow and said, "Where this arrow lands is where you will end up." The arrow landed here, in Iowa, and that is why we came. We followed the arrow in the sky, and we're still on that path today. We're still here, trying hang onto and pass on what remains to our youth. We adapted and adopted another people's way of life and have lost so much in the process. But we believe that this all happened for a reason, that as part of our people's journey, we would come to an almost extinction, and that one day we will find our way back home to where the clay is red.

THE OLD ONES

MY GRANDFATHER was a WWII Navy veteran who met my grandmother at an Indian boarding school in Flandreau, South Dakota. At seventeen, he forged his father's name on his papers and then went to war, while my grandmother returned home after school. When the war was over, they reunited and began their family. They moved around all over the country to work and raise their children. They lived in places like Alaska, where my grandfather learned to fly small planes, and they moved to where the jobs were, like California and Denver. But they found the promise from the Indian Relocation Act was a lie; there was no real advantage to going to the big cities for work. It was also hard to be away from our people. So in the 1970s they decided it was time to return to the Settlement. The Settlement was home, and raising a big family with nine kids was difficult out in the world.

My grandfather initially built a small house-like structure on our homestead. Eventually he built the house I grew up in, a yellow-brown house that sat on top of a hill, and the original structure became a tool and storage shed.

A narrow one-car driveway led to our house from the main road, which I knew growing up as Whiskey Bottom Road. The driveway seemed like a long tunnel of trees enveloping us as we drove up to our house, and I would have to duck branches riding in the back of our pickup truck. We had a neat yard because my grandpa was always doing yard work. He'd tell me it was important take care of our home, that we were fortunate to even have one.

There was a path to our outhouse, which was about 200 feet past the toolshed. The path continued down the hill into the woods, to the main road, and the outhouse was off to the side. Our house had a small porch, and in the winters or on nights when I didn't want to make that long walk to the outhouse, I would pee off the side of the porch. Growing up I was told not to be outside at night, because you don't know what is out there. I was told by our elders that there might be spirits that will mess with you if you are outside at night. Maybe it was just a fable to keep us inside at night and in bed early, but we believed it to be true.

We had a water faucet right outside our house for getting water, and we had a clothes washer next to it with a wringer attached. We had a gas stove for heat, and in the winters my grandparents and I would stand around the stove and get warm.

Over time, my grandfather added more rooms, and as time moved on, so did the improvements to the house. If a house on the Settlement needs maintenance, we call the Tribal Housing Department to take care of it because the tribe as a whole owns the house. Eventually they came and built us a kitchen and bathroom addition with plumbing and water. This was a big deal to us because it meant no more outhouse and hauling water.

On the Settlement, you either grow up with old people or nobody. I grew up with old people. In Meskwaki, *kekyaaki* (pronounced *keh-gyah-hah-gi*) means "old ones" or "old people." Growing up, I was always there like a fly on a wall, listening to the older ones talk. When my grandma and I would visit one of her sisters, they would sit at the kitchen table and drink coffee and smoke cigarettes, and I either had to go outside and play by myself or sit with them and be quiet. There was no other option; there were no other kids around, and I was to be seen and not heard. Sometimes they would give me a piece of bruised fruit.

Eventually I would find myself listening to their stories, often about my relatives going back generations. They spoke about people from the past as if they were still here. I heard their concerns for the language and losing the language. They would say that if we lost our language, we would lose our religion, our way of life, and who we are as a people. But at the same time, they were growing lenient

150

on us younger kids when it came to speaking the language. They spoke half in the language and half in English to us, an indication of the change in times for us as a people.

My grandparents worked at the tribal senior center, so I hung out there a lot. There, all the elders spoke in the Meskwaki language, often playing a game known as bone dice. The game involves a wooden bowl with game pieces carved out of bone. There is a turtle and a bear, and the object is to stand up the bear. If you want in on a round, you throw a penny in a dish. The person who stands up the bear, or gets the most points that round, gets the bowl of pennies. Bone dice being played with a bunch of old Meskwaki women yelling in our language is a sight to see.

My grandparents taught me about our tribal families and who comes from which family. Family is central to Meskwaki life. Our Meskwaki names are recycled—we don't own them, so when we pass on they go back to the clan. Calling each other by our Meskwaki names was highly stressed growing up.

Because I spent most of my time with older people, I had a special connection with them. I gave them my listening ear, my time and attention. In return, they gave me their memories. They gave me the past. They gave me their gems of knowledge. They treated me differently than the other kids. That was the privilege and reward for sitting there during those long evenings.

If I wasn't with my grandparents, I was with my aunts or uncles. I call my first cousins my sisters and brothers because that is how close we are. I spent a lot of time with them, especially my army of sisters, like Quincy, Desse, Anneka, and Alana. Of all the cousins, though, my brother Bill was the one I wanted most to be like.

It wasn't long before I started to realize everyone else had a mom and dad. My cousins next door had a mom and dad. Bill had a mom and dad. And then there was me. I wondered what that could be like, having a mom and dad at home. Mine were never around.

IN THE WOODS AND ON THE ROAD

THE SUMMERTIME is seminal to my memories of growing up. It reminds me of the times I would lie in bed with my grandparents, listening to them speak our language. The birds would be singing outside, and the weeping willows, and I could smell the dew and damp grass, hear the bugs hitting the screen door. I didn't really know how to speak my language, but listening to their words, I knew that I came from a beautiful people. My grandpa would tickle me and say something in Meskwaki, usually about how I was too energetic or always into something, and my grandma would giggle. Sometimes they would throw an English word into their conversation, so I could catch on to what they were saying. I kind of wished the birds would throw in an English word, too, so I could know what they were saying on those summer mornings.

Often those morning talks would be interrupted by noise from our scanner. That's something you should know—everyone on the Settlement seems to have a scanner. We have to know what's going on and who's getting into trouble with the law, and we use it to alert our relatives that the law is looking for them. It's a way to stay one step ahead of the white man. I remember the early summer mornings when I would creep into our back room and listen to the scanner. I can still hear the lady who would screech across the vibe, saying we have a "116 on Highway 30 heading east toward the Settlement." I didn't know then that one day they would be talking about me on the scanner.

Summer was when I got to explore the land. "In the woods" is how we referred to it. My grandma told me to just be home by supper, and then to be inside before dark—and those Iowa summers, the sun didn't go down until ten at night. I would roam to unfamiliar places, following trails and old roads, drifting off into another time and place. I would ride my bike all over, free to go anywhere on the Settlement. I was immersed in trees, thorn bushes, and tall grasses.

On clan ceremony days, my grandma would take her time getting ready, making sure she had on her best earrings and necklace. I would stare out past the backyard into the woods and wish I could be playing in them. It was as if the screen door were a

152

portal to another dimension, my haven.

Summer was also time for our annual powwow, which we have been holding for over a hundred years. The powwow usually takes place the second weekend in August. It began as a religious dance celebrating a good harvest, honoring the plants we hold dear and giving thanks to the Creator for all we have. We sang and danced in the hot Iowa sun for hundreds of years. At the turn of the century we needed a way for the tribe to make money, so we opened it up to the public. We've been performing the same program ever since, the same songs and dances that have been passed down for generations. We still teach our youth these traditions, and every summer we come together and celebrate. We invite our friends and relatives from all over to come celebrate with us and try to maintain good relations with our neighbors.

There were a few years when we didn't have the powwow because many of our relatives were off to war. (Few Americans know that Natives are the highest group of people per capita to serve in the armed forces.) During the Grand Entry of the powwow, veterans lead all the dancers into the arena to start the event. We raise the flags of all the Nations we represent and honor those who have died in combat. We have songs and dances praising these veterans, because that warrior blood lives on in us.

Growing up I also got a glimpse of the world outside rural Iowa by traveling around the surrounding states to powwows with my grandparents. Going to powwows opened my eyes to the many different Natives there are, and their stories taught me what it was like where they were from. At the same time, the stories from the people I met at powwows were similar to mine and were about the same struggles we all endure as Native people. This was a discovery for me, realizing that even though not all Natives are the same, in some ways we are because we share the same struggles. I learned that I was part of a special people and that even though I got treated differently by the non-Natives in Tama, there was a place I could go where I was wanted.

My grandparents had a food stand, and they had traveled to powwows for years selling snow cones and cotton candy and popcorn. They were well known because they were the only ones to sell that kind of food. They hauled around their little trailer, and my aunts danced at the powwows. By the time I came around, I caught the tail end of their dancing, mostly at our local powwow, but their names were still known.

My grandmother encouraged me to go out and dance, and she made me an outfit that resembled a flag. The top was blue with stars and had red and white yarn fringe. The bottom was red and white stripes with fringe. I had a harness and belt, handcuffs, and a headband that were pulled together from other people's outfits or things my grandma had. My head roach was a hand-me-down as well.

I started dancing and singing at a young age at the local powwows in the tribal center gym or the school. I would get ready in the tribal chambers of our governmental building. The gym was attached and was also used as a community space. I remember everyone getting ready around me, throwing on their beadwork and tying up their feather bustles.

I started out as a fancy feather dancer but found my groove as a grass dancer. Where the fancy dancer is fast on their feet, quick and athletic, the grass dancer is smooth, sliding feet, swaying with beat. Getting lost in the grass dance was one of the first ways I learned to express myself through art.

BETWEEN TWO WORLDS

MY UPBRINGING CONSISTED OF BOTH the traditional Meskwaki way of life and the modern American world. Entering the '80s, I adapted with the times and became interested in more modern parts of life. In 1986 I woke up to the greatest Christmas present a kid could ever ask for, a Nintendo Entertainment System. I will always remember that morning because I slept on a couch with a pullout bed next to the gas stove, which was turned up to offset the treacherous Iowa winters and cold concrete floors. Light snuck in through a crack in the yellowish canvas curtains, and our tree was lit up off to the side.

A few years later, we got a satellite dish and were able to watch all the cable channels via satellite dish. My favorite channel was The Box, a music video channel where you could dial a phone number to play a video. It was cool because you could play hip-hop videos all day long. That was how I got ahead of everyone with my knowledge of hip-hop, by always watching The Box. I also liked watching boxing with my grandfather. We were big fans, so when the major fights were transitioning from NBC and ABC to cable, we caught them on the satellite dish.

Even though technology was coming into our lives in small ways, my grandparents were still old school. We had kerosene lamps for when storms came and the lights went out. Sometimes it was better to sit in the dark with my grandparents and listen to them talk about the old days, which usually ended in talking about our Meskwaki traditions.

From a young age, my grandparents told me about our way of life and our role as members of the Thunder Clan. When strong storms came, they would tell me to put out tobacco, our sacrament, so the storms would go by calmly. Tobacco is sacred to most indigenous cultures in North America—pure tobacco, not Marlboro cigarette tobacco. We Meskwaki offer it when we pray each day, our traditional way of connecting with the Creator. It is used as an offering to the spirits for whatever you prayed for, such as to calm the storms. Because we have children, women, and elderly among us, we ask the storms to go by quietly so as not to startle or scare them. When the meteorologist shows the Doppler radar of our area during a severe storm, it always seems to go around the Settlement, and we know that's why.

In the early '80s, we were slowly influenced by the outside world, and my grandfather would tell me that we needed to be twice as smart as the white man because we needed to know how to operate in both worlds. Times were changing, and my tribe entered the world of gaming by opening a bingo hall. It was so successful that eventually we opened a full-service casino. Our gaming business would change our lives as a people forever in both good and bad ways. It definitely changed the way the non-Natives in the area felt about us.

Our casino allowed us to take care of ourselves without help from outsiders, including our own health, education, and legal systems geared toward our way of life as a sovereign nation. However, it also changed who we are as a people. We once were a people who didn't believe in the American capitalist system, a people who hadn't truly been colonized and still believed in and practiced our old ways. Going from that to a billion-dollar casino had an impact, and it all came so fast that we had to adjust quickly. Suddenly, we went from poverty to receiving more money than we had ever seen. Dividend checks went to shareholders—each enrolled Meskwaki. At the height of the casino success, in the '80s and '90s before the recession, each member was receiving monthly bonus payments of thousands of dollars. I didn't get the payments in the beginning because enrollment came though your father and mine didn't recognize me, but a few years later a DNA test established paternity, and I was able to enroll and begin receiving my checks.

We didn't know what to do with all that money. We stopped our Native practices like gardening and started shopping at malls and grocery stores. We could afford alcohol and drugs and started buying them. We started to emulate the stars we saw on TV. Our work ethic dropped. Why work three jobs if we didn't have to? Poor people getting all of that money—we didn't know how to manage it. Plus, the world around us was changing so quickly with technology. We were trying to be part of a system that wasn't ours.

Five miles east of our house was Tama, a railroad town where we could take care of most of our business because it had a post office, bank, grocery store, bar—all the typical things you can find in small-town Iowa. A railroad connected Tama to Toledo, a more upscale town just to the north.

These two towns were divided by the railroad line, but that wasn't all that divided them. The kids from both towns went to school together. Some kids from Toledo wouldn't associate with kids from Tama because they felt they were above them. You can learn a lot about a place from its kids and schools. And there was a difference not only between the kids from the two towns, but also the kids from the country, or the farm kids, and us, the Meskwaki.

The divide between the two towns grew worse after the success of the casino. There was this hatred because people believed it

156

wasn't fair that we Natives were able to find a way to come out of our situation. They failed to understand the history of the country forgetting about us and leaving us high and dry for many years. When we found a way to get on our feet, many people didn't like that.

On the other hand, there were white families who slowly became okay with Meskwakis once we started getting money from the casino. Suddenly we could afford better shoes and clothes and gear for sports. We could afford the things the white kids had. I still remember when I bought my first pair of Jordans.

Non-Natives were starting to hang out with us Meskwakis more, and I was being invited to birthday parties and going out with girls from town. Their parents didn't always like it, but they kept it to themselves. It was becoming more acceptable to be friends with us because we had grown out of poverty. When our socioeconomic status came up, it was easier to accept us.

Growing up in "central Iowa" didn't mean anything to me as a kid. I felt distant from the stories of the area because our story wasn't part of them. Everything had been manipulated by historians who had come to document us on their terms. To me, we were the real Iowans. All that mattered to me was that I was from a place where the songs were still sung and the corn was still being planted, and us kids were hearing the language of our ancestors. I had my woods to escape to, and I had my love of art to keep me company.

THE ESCAPE ARTIST

MY MOM WAS IN and out of my life, and I didn't really know my dad. At the time, I didn't know how to say, "I miss my mom." I was trying to understand why I wasn't important enough to be loved by my mom and dad. I had my grandparents and was happy with them, but deep inside, I was angry and sad. I felt worthless. At school, I had trouble listening. I got mad when I couldn't understand an assignment and would give up or start messing with other students.

Sometimes classmates would say things to me and provoke a

confrontation, like telling me to go back where I came from. They knew I'd be the one to get punished because I had a history of getting into trouble. Eventually the teachers stuck me in closets for time-outs. When I got worse, they separated me from the other students, and I had a special teacher, a Native state wrestling champ, to monitor me so I wouldn't get into fights.

My grandparents knew what was happening at school, but parenting had changed for them over the years. They were strict, as my grandfather was in the military, but they also let a lot of things slide. They were more explanatory in their teachings, more guides than disciplinarians. For instance, they would let me know what would happen if I did something wrong and how I shouldn't be misbehaving. However, I think they understood the way I felt, being without parents.

I craved attention and found that when I misbehaved, I got the attention I sought from my peers. I acted out because I didn't know how to deal with these emotions I had building up, which would later get me into trouble in more ways than one. When my grandparents were too lenient, my uncle took over as a parental figure. He took me in at times and disciplined me by having me do chores like raking the leaves and picking up the trash that roaming dogs spread everywhere.

Part of my uncle's way of teaching me how to behave involved bringing me to ceremonial preparations. I had to sit there and be quiet and listen to the men who would lead the ceremonies. I had to work—haul wood, haul water, sharpen knives, and tend the fire. One time my community was having a powwow at the gym, and I couldn't attend because I was in trouble and had to go with my uncle to help prepare for the next day's ceremony. I was sad because I always felt like I was in trouble and like everything I did was wrong, yet I felt powerless to change.

Living with older people was different because they had an older way of raising a child. I either had to play outside or sit still and be quiet. It was fun going to other people's houses, because I felt like I was part of a family and had a bunch of brother and sisters. Eventually, though, I would have to go back home where it was just me. That was where I had to devise my own ways to escape.

158

After a long day of playing outside and coming in for the night, I would go to my room and listen to powwow music and draw, look at magazines, or write poetry, inspired by my mom. She was attending the Institute of American Indian Arts, or IAIA, in Santa Fe to get her degree in creative writing. She was a young mother, and my grandparents told her to go have her college experience while they took care of me. I used to look through her art and writing books from the school. Flipping through the pages of Native designs and drawings of Native men with feathers, suns, and geometric stars dotting the background, fading into the pages, I would think about how I wished I could be part of her world and her art.

I remember one evening in particular when I was ten years old. I sat there drawing, thinking about everything going on in a ten-year-old's world. My thoughts were swerving in and out of the right lane, from the absence of my mother to being bullied on the bus to being teased at school by the white kids to the occasional bullying by kids at the Tribal Center, who teased me because I didn't have siblings and because I had big ears. Drawing was how I escaped from all of those things on my mind.

I was getting better at the cartoon characters I was drawing, inspired by my older brother Bill. He wasn't my biological brother but the son of my aunt, which you now know in Meskwaki structure is considered my brother. My interest in art was growing, and he was the only person I knew who was like me and into the same things.

Bill was a few years older than me. He was funny and a jokester, into sports, basketball, card collecting, and movies. Just like a big brother, he knew all the cool things. He was good at building things and remote control cars. He was so creative, he could come up with anything on the spot. Most importantly, though, he was an artist. When he would share his paintings and drawings with me, I wanted to be like him. I remember we would have drawing sessions at the kitchen table at my aunt's house where I would trace his work and try to figure out how to draw like him.

My desire to impress Bill with my art became an obsession. I wanted to have something for the next time I went to my aunt's house that he would say was cool. While I sketched, though, I couldn't help thinking about how much I missed my mom. Why wasn't she with me? I didn't even know where she was some of the time. Drawing through the pain was how I maintained as a kid. All of these thoughts built up the more I touched lead to paper, but I couldn't let them out. I wasn't supposed to be weak. We Meskwakis were warriors.

My grandparents encouraged my mom and me to have a relationship, and we would try, but her drinking and not wanting to give up the party life kept her away. I knew she was my mom, but she never acted like it. When they would tell me I was going to stay with my mom, I felt like I was sleeping over at someone's house. I would come home on Sunday.

As I grew older, I got tired of waiting for her to pick me up. I remember sitting on our couch, excited for her to come, watching and waiting as the TV stations ran through their nightly shows. On Sundays Disney movies played in the evenings, and I sat there watching the movie, keeping track of the time based on scenes in the movie. Car lights were noticeable as soon as somebody turned off Whiskey Bottom Road, and as the movie ended, I realized no lights had appeared. I knew she wasn't coming. I went into my room, took out my sketch pad, and started drawing.

Once, my grandparents and I drove down to the Institute in Santa Fe to visit my mom. She took me on a tour of the campus, where I saw people making pottery on spinning wheels. It was a good visit, but then it was over and we came home. A few years later, she came back to Iowa. She had gotten some money, and she bought a car. She told me we were going to move to Albuquerque together. My uncle lived down there with his family. We bought a new stereo and some CDs, and then we packed up our stuff and headed south. Throughout all of this, staying with her was hard because I knew it was only a matter of time before she found a reason to bounce and I would live with my grandparents again. Eventually I hit my breaking point, and I vowed to never let anybody hurt me again.

TRYING TO BECOME A MAN

I HAD MY FIRST DRINK at twelve years old. I thought I was grown. I thought I was a man. I felt on my own. We stole someone's mom's beer and drank it in the woods. I liked to drink. It was like a rite of passage. I felt like a Native man. There were always alcoholics around me, and it felt like finally I got to take that step and be like the other men. That was what we did. We were Natives. We drank.

It was the beginning of my adolescence. I was not listening to my grandparents, and I had started testing my limits with their rules and getting into trouble at school. I thought I knew it all. My grandparents were doing what they could to keep me on the right track, explaining to me how I was going down the wrong path and trying to steer me back. They made me go live with my uncle at times, but I always went back home.

The high school years were different. The town was changing. The world around us was changing. I was changing. Our lives were defined by the success of our casino. The early '90s also brought an influx of Hispanic people to Iowa seeking a better life. Now, not only did the townspeople not like having us Meskwaki around, they had a whole other group of brown folks moving in. That kind of environment drew us outsiders closer together, and new relationships formed in the community. There was also growing tension at high school events, and fights began to break out.

There was so much tension at school, there was a walkout, and there were gun threats, which made it even harder for me to go to school. Around that time, I learned of another option. A few of my older cousins had taken off to this school in Flandreau, South Dakota. It was an all-Indian boarding school, the same one my grandparents attended. I had never thought of being away from home, and the idea was enticing. My cousins told me stories about how Natives from all over the country went there. I thought it would be a good time to get away from the problems at home, so I went.

Flandreau was a little town with stores, a Pizza Ranch, and its own history. Because my older cousins were already there, it wasn't like I was going somewhere unfamiliar. But it was my first time away from home. I had gone to basketball camps and church camps for the weekends and traveled to powwows, but I was never away from my community for long. I was going to be in Flandreau for months, miles away from home.

Flandreau was its own world, an island in the middle of nowhere. There were people from all kinds of tribes. Many were from bigger cities, and some were people I'd met on the powwow trail. It was easy to jump in with the crowd because my older cousins had already been there for a while. I fit right in.

By the time I came to Flandreau, I knew that the world around me wasn't for me. The history of Native people and white people, Tama-Toledo and the racism there—it was all still in my mind. I had to find something I could relate to, and fortunately I did: hip-hop.

Hip-hop culture had a strong presence at the school. A lot of the people listened to hip-hop and R&B music. We dressed in Karl Kani, represented sports teams, wore our hats backward. Some people came from Chicago, and they would rap, and there were some girls who could sing. They would post up by the cafeteria area and just start performing. I had another friend from Chicago who could do graffiti.

I still remember the first time I heard Wu-Tang Clan and how their music spoke to me. Hip-hop culture was like me—not well received. To many people, it was noise, foreign, a fad, something they wished would go away. But I could relate to the stories of feeling alone and feeling like the world is against you. From an early age, I noticed how similar our Native struggles were to the African-American struggles, even in the Midwest. I learned how people in our community felt about not only Natives but all people of color. Social injustice, racism, poverty, hopelessness, struggling with the effects of colonization, living in America—we lived on parallel tracks, moving together, yet we were different. No struggle outweighs the other—we are both the water, the earth, and the fire, walking on our ancestors' bones—but I could see the similarities between African Americans and us, and because of those similarities, their music spoke to me.

I continued to have problems in classes because I didn't take

162

them seriously. I was more concerned with being somebody than I was with doing well in school. I would finish my work fast and clown around the rest of the time. I often got in trouble with the teachers, and when authority came down on me, I acted out some more. I still carried the feelings of sadness and loneliness inside me, and I didn't know how to deal with them. I didn't think guys were supposed to talk about our feelings because it made us look weak. I couldn't look weak because I felt I had to prove something, that I was tough and a survivor. I felt I had to be that way to protect myself so no one could hurt me.

Playing basketball had been an escape for me in Iowa, keeping me in the spirit of trying and on a better path, so I joined the team at Flandreau. That kept me going for a while. But I was still attracted to that other life and hanging out with that wrong crowd, and I shortly found myself kicked out of Flandreau for misbehaving. So, back to Iowa and town school I went.

I would go back and forth between Flandreau and Iowa again, succumbing to the same problems. My grandparents were let down, but they simply stressed that I was going to have a tough life if I didn't change my ways. They never judged me, though, or left me hanging. They just wanted me to do right. Deep down, though, it hurt me when I disappointed them. And when they didn't punish me, I felt even worse. I didn't know how to deal with those feelings, so I did the only thing I knew how to do—I held them all in and acted out. It was only a matter of time until I went too far.

THE DARK NIGHT

MY GRANDPARENTS HAD GONE south for the winter, leaving me home by myself. I was sixteen and had not been in school. I had been traveling around with my friend to powwows, and when I wasn't doing that, I was at home on the Settlement or in Tama messing around. It was winter. I was drinking and doing drugs at this time in my life, and I was pretty distant from my family. I came and went as I pleased, not telling my grandparents where I was going or who I was going with or when I was coming back.

Nobody could tell me anything. It seemed like everything I did, I got into trouble. But trouble had become a way for me to both seek attention and to protect myself—be violent and people will leave you alone and not hurt you. I thought that if I didn't have a heart or feelings, then nobody could hurt me emotionally, either. Protecting myself was my priority, because all I had was myself. Society—the cops, the courts, the schools, the townspeople, the farmers—didn't like Native people. School couldn't teach me anything. I had grown up being told by teachers that something was wrong with me because I had behavioral problems and that I belonged in closets, away from people, alone.

So, at sixteen, my attitude was terrible and my outlook was shot. I knew I was never going to be anything. I had seen how it was accepted in my community to be an alcoholic and to act the way I did, and the people I was hanging around with encouraged it. I always felt like I had to prove something to somebody, to gain that attention and love I didn't get from my parents. I felt like I had to live up to my peers' expectations in order for them to accept me. My brother Bill wasn't into the things that I was doing; he had a mom and dad, so he had that fear of a whooping. He had art and sports, and he was a good kid. But I wasn't like him. I was another kind of kid.

I had been sitting at home by myself for a few days, depressed, because nobody had come to check me out. I had been living off frozen pizza, pop, and chips, and I was out of drugs. So one Friday afternoon when I heard a car pulling up and someone shouting, "Let's go!", I went.

It was clear that everyone had been drinking already—nothing out of the norm, because that was the life we lived. As I got in the van, a bottle of Jim Beam was handed to me, and I was instructed to take a shot. I obliged. We backed out of my driveway and started the evening driving around the back roads. The plan was to head into Tama to find some girls to hang out with. We drove around and drank until it got dark. I kept drinking more and more.

Looking back, I remember how when I was getting ready to go, I had this feeling that I should stay home, that I didn't really want to go out. I had found a comfort in being home alone, sad and

164

depressed. But I didn't listen to that voice. I went.

There are holes in my memories of that night—everything was blurry, riding around and drinking. At one point I was walking down a street in Tama, cold and wet. I went to the house of a girl I knew who partied. Everyone there was asleep, and I remember them telling me to leave because I was drunk and being stupid. I don't know what time it was, but the streets were empty and everything was closed. I remember wanting to walk home, down the train tracks. That was the safest way home, without the cops messing with you, although many people have been hit by trains on those tracks.

I don't remember anything after that. Everything went black.

I woke up lying by a phone booth. A cop had been trying to wake me up. There was blood all over me. Suddenly I was in the back of his car. Then I was in a room with bright lights. My clothes were soaked through.

I honestly don't know what happened that night. I was told some friends and I had gotten into a fight with a guy we didn't know. They told me I went into a rage and used a metal object to beat him. He didn't die, but he was hurt badly.

The district attorney wanted to make an example out of me, and he did. He charged me as an adult at sixteen years old. I had never been sent to juvenile home, but I had a history of fighting at school, and they used that to prove I was grown enough to face adult charges.

My family was devastated. I wasn't taught to act that way. My grandparents raised me to be a good person, and I had gone off the path. My grandparents and my mom were also afraid of what could happen to me in the system. Everyone convinced me to take a plea bargain, ten years for willful injury. They said that since I was young, I would get out when I was eighteen. Later I would find out that is not how the system works for adult sentencing. Ultimately I would end up serving over three years plus two on parole, but they could have kept me my entire sentence if they wanted to.

I was sixteen years old and sitting in the back of a transport vehicle. The radio was on as the officer drove east down Highway

30, and as I watched the Iowa landscape pass—trees, fields, barns, farmsteads—I felt I was watching my youth pass as well.

I didn't know it at the time, but my life was about to change drastically. I thought I was going to Eldora, or to Clarinda to a youth center. But when they charge you as an adult, you go to prison. Eldora was northwest of Tama, and I was heading east, to a place called Oakdale. A federal prison.

When we pulled up to the metal gate, I wasn't really afraid. I didn't know what to expect. I'd lived a rough life already and had seen some things, but I didn't have anybody in my direct family who had been to prison. I knew of people who had been there, and I'd heard stories, but I had never been locked up. I heard the metal gates begin to slide across the cold frozen youth of my life. As we drove forward, I entered a new life, one that would break me and then shape me.

IN THE SYSTEM

THERE WAS A COT and a toilet and a metal desk covered with writing by other people—dates and times, people's names repeated. I remember thinking, "I don't want to come back here and see my name scratched into this table." It was cold. Brick and metal. All I could hear was the air coming in.

The lights were on. People were yelling. The jailer came by. It smelled like garbage and sadness.

After two years at Oakdale, they moved me to the Newton Correctional Facility.

Different people, but the setup was the same: concrete room, metal bed, toilet, sink. It was cold and miserable. The writing was on the walls. You know your sentence and how long you are going to be there.

I grew up in prison. I wasn't in gangs. I wasn't a snitch. I wasn't involved with the prison scene—I hadn't grown in up the system, and I didn't have friends there like some people did. I kept to myself or hung out with other Natives. I started to draw again.

At first, when my mom said she would come to visit, I didn't believe her. But then she came. I remember thinking, "Are you trying to be my mom now? Because it's too late."

It didn't last.

She would call on the prison phone. I'd call her back to talk.

"Well, I planned on coming to visit you this weekend," she'd begin. And I'd let myself believe.

In prison you couldn't talk to just anybody. Having a visitor was something to look forward to. Those Saturdays I would get ready, and I'd wait. And wait. I'd eventually realize she wasn't coming. Finally I couldn't take it anymore, and I told her, "Don't come at all. It's too late."

It's true that in jail, you find prayer and God.

You think about your life. You have a lot of time on your hands.

I had to face the truth. I was a felon. A violent felon. There was no hope for me.

People who had been in and out of institutions their whole lives told me I was young and needed to straighten out. But I knew my life was over. All I had at that point was prayer.

When you pray, you pray for others first. Then you pray for yourself. Pray for good health and specific things.

You have to be careful when you pray. You have to be careful how you word it, because it could be interpreted wrong, and you might not receive that blessing. You have to mean it, and it has to come from your heart, not your brain.

I prayed for sick people, for elderly people, for my grandparents—I was always afraid that they would die while I was away. I prayed to be a better man. To not hurt people. To not say bad things about people or think bad things about people. I prayed to see life the way our Creator intended.

WORKING THE PROGRAM

WHEN I GOT OUT of prison in December 1999, I went to a work release center in Des Moines. A work release center is where you go to transition into society after being incarcerated. You have to get a job or go to school, attend substance-abuse meetings like

Alcoholics Anonymous, and basically behave. My mother lived in Des Moines, and when I was making my decision to get out, I didn't want to go back into the same environment. So, I went to Des Moines and worked the program.

My first AA meeting was in Des Moines after I'd gotten out of prison. You go in there thinking you have to tell your whole life that first time. I'm a quiet person, and I sat there and just listened. I thought, why the hell am I here? But I had to go three times a week, and I did.

I went to AA around Des Moines here and there, just to get my paper slip signed. Then someone told me about a Native meeting at a hospital on Saturdays. So I went, and that's where I met the Native guy who ran the meeting. He worked for the Homeless Youth Center, and he was cool with me and talked to me a lot about making that transition back into the world. He would take me to lunch and show me what he did at the shelter, eventually finding me some jobs.

I had young cousins in Des Moines, and one night they came to take me out. There were seven of us, sitting around the shelter at a park. The beer came out. We were laughing and talking. I was the new guy, and people were asking about me, what I did and where I was from.

Then someone asked me if I wanted a beer. My cousin looked at me. Time stopped. I could see him thinking, wondering what I was going to do. My fingers shook. I knew I could drink and nothing would happen. If no one found out, I wouldn't get in trouble or go back to prison. But I remembered what they said in AA, that it could lead me back to where I had been. I didn't want to go back to that place.

"No, thanks. I've got stuff to do in the morning," I said.

They said okay, they understood, they had jobs too. The moment passed.

After that, the things I had been hearing in AA stayed in my head. I was in a new place and I wanted to make friends, but I always remembered everything I had to lose.

I chose to attend school at DMACC, the Des Moines Area

Community College. This was a big change from the way I had grown up, but I didn't want my experience to hinder my life. It was hard, and I had to get used to being around young people. Most of the time I felt older than my actual age of nineteen. I also got a job, working at a music store at Merle Hay Mall. The Disc Jockey had tapes, VCR movies, CDs, DVDs, the whole nine. I was a sales clerk.

I was always nervous. I would go to class, then to work, and then back to the work release center. My mom and I had built a relationship while I was in prison, and she gave me rides and helped me out. She lived in Johnston, so that's where I would take my furloughs home. Furloughs started with a few hours on the weekend, then increased with good behavior to full weekends and finally to getting released.

The first chance I got to go home, my family came up to visit. We had a small gathering with my grandparents and a few others. We cooked out and visited. I got to go into my own room and bathroom.

The first visit was a short one, but eventually as my time increased, Bill made it up to see me. It was crazy to see him because we had only talked on the phone from time to time. He had grown into his own self but was still the same to me. We smoked cigarettes and talked about everything that had happened up until that point. I showed him my guitars, which I taught myself to play in prison. It was great to finally be around my people again, but I was a kid the last time everyone saw me. They didn't know what I had gone through or how I was feeling inside. Because in a way, you do get comfortable being in prison. You grow into a routine. You know what to expect, and you don't have to worry about the outside world.

Bill would say some serious things in our talks. He wanted me to stay out of trouble and get my life together. But we also talked about partying when I was off parole. Even though I was doing good, part of me was angry at what happened, and part of me was depressed. Part of me was also gone forever—those teenage years. The times when I was supposed to be tearing it up in high school basketball or going to prom, maybe finding that high school sweetheart or falling in love with that beautiful Canadian fancy shawl dancer.

Instead, I was a violent felon. My life was over, and there was no reason for me to exist. I definitely wasn't going to make it in this world, because once people knew my past, they were going to judge me even more.

I was making strides toward getting out of the work release center, but from there I went on parole for another two years. While on parole, you are free to do whatever you want, but if you mess up, you go back to prison. The music store closed and I had to find another job, which I did, working for a place that made windows. All I wanted was to be free again. But for the time being, I had to play the game.

A NEW PATH

I WAS RELEASED from parole a few months early for good behavior. But after I had been off for a while, I didn't go to AA meetings anymore. Without the threat of a parole officer or the state, I felt free. I decided to drink again. I knew it had just put me through three years of hell, but that was the power of addiction.

I had been talking to this girl back home, an old girlfriend from high school, and she had been coming to Des Moines to see me. One night when she came to visit, we had made plans to party. I was nervous because I was used to everything I did being under a microscope, but in a way, I had been waiting for this moment, thinking that I deserved to have a fun night.

After that, I began drinking again. I moved back home after a while and met the girl who would later have my children. Upon the birth of my first son, in 2003, I knew I had to get my life together. I wanted to have a family, but my alcoholism ate away at my outlook and attitude toward myself and toward life.

As my family grew, my alcoholism grew, too. I still wouldn't grow up and continued to be in and out of jail. I was a toxic partner to the mother of my children. I was trapped in that cycle that has messed up Native families for generations. The more I continued to drink, the more I wanted to not be on Earth anymore. Even with all the beautiful blessings I had in life, I still was stuck on what I had done and what I had gone through. I felt like because I kept making mistakes and digging myself into a deeper hole, I was worthless.

In the midst of all of this, I could hear in my head my grandparents, and my uncle, and the Meskwaki way of life telling me otherwise. I made an effort to do right and change my life, and there were times when I did do well, when I went to school and was a family man and got active in my community. But alcohol kept pushing me down.

I had period after period of sobriety, but I was always going back to my old ways. It wasn't only an alcohol problem, either. I'd gone to prison for being violent. I'd never addressed that part of me. It was my protection. People knew I was violent, so they'd leave me alone. When I got out of prison and back into the world, I thought that part of me would go away, but it was still there. I thought that in choosing to make a new life, those things would stay in the past. But they came back uglier than ever.

I had been taught never to hurt women. I grew up around mostly women, other than my grandfather and uncle. But abuse was always around. At any Native party, there was domestic violence. Boys would push around their girlfriends, we would break it up, and we would move on. It wasn't just men, either; it was women too. When we drank, it came out like an explosion.

In my first relationship, I was abusive. She was a good girl, smart, and she loved me, but she was an alcoholic too. The basis of our relationship was alcohol. I pushed people away by drinking. If they engaged me physically or put their hands on me while I was drunk, I would get violent. We were toxic together. We had three children, so this went on for a while. We were living together, trying to make it work. I was also trying to get sober, but I knew we couldn't get sober together. Finally, after much turmoil, we decided it was over. She was angry and left with the kids to go to school and have a better life.

One day I had gotten out of jail for the umpteenth time and was sitting around my house, upset, disappointed, and giving up on life. At the same time, I was also feeling like I couldn't give up. I sighed and looked out the window to clear my head, wondering what I wanted to do with my life. I paced around my living room and kitchen, trying to figure out how I could change my life and break the cycle of doing good and then messing up and going to jail. I wanted to live for my children, but I was a screw-up.

Finally, I prayed. When I opened my eyes, I came to the conclusion that I was only good at one thing: art. It was the one thing that had been there for me throughout everything. I always had a paper and pen, even while I was in prison. Now I just had to find my medium. Being a painter was typical for Native artists, and I didn't want to be like everybody else, so I chose fashion. I'd also always wanted to do tattoos, and I thought that through clothing, people could wear my art, kind of like a tattoo.

Once I established that I wanted to do fashion, I had to come up with a name. I spent hours sketching out different ideas and meanings. I believed that if I was going to do something, I wanted it to have a purpose, and I finally came up with Daepian: Drive Ambition Empowerment Progression In All Natives. This endeavor would change my life, as I discovered that I couldn't talk about those characteristics and not live them.

I was doing well on my own, but eventually I met a girl. I was in a good place and wanted to try being in a relationship again. Once we were together, I realized she was an alcoholic. And once I was around it, the cycle began again.

We had our daughter right away. I felt I had to stay and raise my child, but things spiraled quickly to a toxic place. Her family got involved. Drugs were part of her life. I had been sure I could change, but I was bound to this relationship through our daughter and then our son.

Drink and fight was our cycle. One weekend, we were on our third day of drinking. We were at her brothers' house, which wasn't common because he and I didn't get along. We started to fight, but I was stronger and older than him, so I took off. Later she showed up, used an ID to break into my house. I told her to leave and it escalated. I remember opening the door to tell her to leave, and she pushed me. I held her down and told her she didn't want me to get angry. She took the keys to my car and left.

Four days later the police came to my house from three different departments: Tama, Toledo, and Meskwaki. I was charged with

172

assault and airway obstruction. Although I was a violent person and was willing to take responsibility for my actions, I felt the story didn't reflect the truth. So we went to court, but a jury found me guilty. It would be my second felony charge.

I was not sentenced for a year. During that summer, I traveled around the country selling my clothing and launching my business. I wanted that life, a life where I wasn't in trouble, where I was a normal person.

The final straw was the night of my cousin's wedding in Des Moines. I had a few post-wedding drinks, and then walking out of a bar, I was arrested for public intoxication. Once again, I had to call home and tell someone I was in jail.

The next day, October 6, 2013, I decided I was done. It was the last day I ever had a drink of alcohol. I didn't want to die, but I didn't want to continue living the way I was living. I knew I was a better person than that, because I knew where I had come from. I had just gotten out of jail for the millionth time. My relationships with the mothers of my children had failed, which devastated me. I wanted to be a family man and create something I never had. But I was an alcoholic and a felon two times over, and I felt like my life was over yet again.

The Creator was asking me, do you want to continue, or have you had enough?

I told the Creator, whatever I have to do, I'll do it, please just make it stop.

I made a plan to change my entire life. I was desperate to return to the person I knew I was inside. I wanted to be that little kid again, the one who played in the woods, who was open and full of life. I wanted to be an artist. I wanted to be a basketball player. I wanted to reclaim that sixteen-year-old boy and show people the real me. The real me is caring and has a heart. The real me is goofy and a clown and can make people laugh.

I had seen bits and pieces of a good life, and through my children, I had experienced real love. My children showed me that my presence was important to them. I needed to give them a great father, because I didn't have one. I wanted to be somebody they could look up to, as I did my grandfather. I wanted to be the kind of man he was. And my grandparents were getting older and were starting to have health issues, and I wanted to honor them and the way they raised me by growing up and living the way they taught me. At the age of twenty-eight, I decided to change my life not only because of my children and my grandparents, but also because I realized that I was somebody to myself, too.

The following year, 2014, was my year of awakening. I didn't know it at the time, but it would be my one-eighty. I realized I had met people who had turned their lives around and were successful, and maybe I could do the same.

In October of 2014 I was sentenced to a year in prison for my second felony. But this time was different. I went in with the outlook that I would make the most of my time. While I was in, I returned to AA and decided to take it seriously. I read the books, I talked at meetings, I let it all out. I did so well, they asked me to start leading meetings.

When I got out, I started an AA meeting in my community. I gathered it at the senior center, the same center where my grandparents used to work. We had a nice group, five to eight people I still follow up with today.

I also started to volunteer. I joined the powwow committee, and I was the powwow emcee a couple of years. I worked numerous jobs in my community.

I started to read a lot. I was looking for a way to deal with my emotions, and I stumbled on a book by Deepak Chopra, *The Seven Spiritual Laws of Success*, that talked about a different approach to getting well, by finding happiness through a constant state of love and compassion. I had never read anything like it before, never thought life could be that way.

I also read about the relationship between animals and the planet. At the time, my sister and I were working out and trying to lose weight. She told me we should try to be vegetarians. I took it even further and became a vegan.

I wanted to be the father I'd seen in so many men, the father I never had, a father whose kids could depend on him. I knew that for everyone to depend on me, especially my kids and my grandparents, I would have to stay on my new path no matter how hard it got.

THE FUNERAL

STANDING IN THE COLD January wind at the burial grounds with my aunts and uncles, my cousins, and my children at my side, it hit me that this would be the last day I would physically see the man who made me who I am. All the years we put in together, teacher–student, grandfather–grandson, were over. The man I'd known as a father had made his way to the next part of his journey, no longer to suffer with us here on this beautiful Earth. The man who would wake up every winter morning to take me to basketball practice, who would sit and listen to me even when I had lost my way, who had grown old before my eyes—my war hero, my boxer, my pilot—was no longer with me. And Bill had recently passed, too, leaving us only a year and a half earlier. Even though our relatives aren't truly gone to us when they die, only a spiritual call away, I still miss going home and seeing Grandpa sitting on the couch or scooting by in the kitchen, smiling at me, saying "Hooah!"

Standing there at his grave, it hit me that I needed to do something more with my life, because my team was passing on. My grandfather had taught me everything I needed to know to be a good man. On that freezing day in the middle of winter, mourning his passing, I recalled those summer mornings lying in bed with my grandparents. I was a child again, listening to the woods come alive, hearing the weeping willows whistle while the dew on the grass glistened. The sun crept through the trees, and my grandparents spoke our Meskwaki language. I knew that no matter what, I had been blessed with good people to guide me through this crazy world.

I looked over at my grandmother and said a prayer of thanks to still be graced with her beautiful presence. And then and there, I decided to go back to college.

A FUTURE FOR THE RED EARTH PEOPLE

THE WOOD-PANEL CURTAIN sits at an angle, dangling from the window seal, as the sun shines on the apartment buildings across the street and the leaves on the bushes outside the glass wiggle around. Lying in my bed looking out the window, past all of that sky, I notice clouds floating across the light blue canvas and think about how far my life has come. Soon I'll graduate from University of Iowa with an art degree and an entrepreneurial management certificate, a dream of mine.

Being a nontraditional student, in my late 30s and going back to school, isn't the ideal way a person should live, according to most Americans. A person is expected to graduate high school, go to college, get a good job, get married, and then have kids. My elders would say that us younger people do things backward—we have kids first, then get a job, go to school, and so on. I am a father of six children and have lived many lives before I arrived here on the UI campus. But I made it.

Life for me has always been like a storm brewing. Gradually changing, moving, energy building up and then unleashing. Morphing and changing, I roll with the punches. I put out my tobacco, and I pray every day.

When my grandfather passed away in 2017, I decided I needed to get on my own two feet because he left me some big shoes to fill. I have gone through so much healing and self-work since I decided to get sober, mainly because I wanted to be a great father to my children. I wanted to be somebody they could look up to, similar to what I had in my grandparents.

I also wanted to be there for my grandmother. I've had the privilege and honor of taking care of my grandparents as they aged, in particular my grandfather for several years as he dealt with illness. After he passed on, I decided to go back and get my associate's degree at community college, where I only needed to take one more class. When I was talking to an advisor and she said I could go to any school, I chose the school I always dreamed of attending: the University of Iowa.

Living a sober life is going to be a lifelong fight. I am cool with that, because I have family. I have my ancestors behind me, and I know I can live the good life that they prayed for us to have.

In telling my story, I wanted to share with young people in particular all that I went through growing up, and that despite the mistakes I made, I survived. I don't want kids to feel hopeless, or that their life has no value, or that nobody cares. I want them to know that no matter what, if they want to change their life, they can. I prayed for a better life. It wasn't easy—I had to get sober, had to change my attitude and way of thinking. I had to atone for what I'd done. You have to do the work. You can't expect the prayers to do all the work for you. You have to meet them halfway. If you do, changing your life is possible.

The road here hasn't always been easy, some of it due to society and some due to my own choices—substance abuse, incarceration, failed relationships, living in two worlds, racism, violence, growing up a Native in America. I experienced violence as a child and didn't grow up with parents. I don't know my language, and I don't know my traditional way of life like I should. I grew up in a system that wasn't designed to see Native people succeed or flourish. In telling my story, I wanted to show people another kind of Iowa childhood, one that was not always pretty. Growing up in a small town with racism and prejudice had an effect on me. And I wanted to share that despite the problems you've faced, no matter where you are from or where you are now, you can change your situation.

Not only can you change yourself, but the people around you can change, too. My mom and I have a good relationship today. She is proud of me and the path I am on now. She knows she messed up, but she was there for me when I needed her most, and she continues to be there for me as well as for my children. I think she's proud that I turned out to be an artist and activist, because she is where I get that from. I am who I am because of her.

I also wanted to educate people about the history of Iowa and its land. I wanted to share the beauty that this land once was. I wanted to show that I come from a culture that has been here for a long time, and that we honor what our ancestors set forth for us many years ago: to live here and raise our children, plant our crops, and practice our religion. We still hold our annual Corn Celebration and invite the community to be part of our culture for one week out of the summer. For over a hundred years, we have been doing this to show that we want to continue to be good cohabitants with our fellow Iowans.

I grew up with a rich history and culture. I love my people. I love being at the *otenikani* with my uncles. I love sitting at the kitchen table with my grandmother. I loved my grandfather telling me about life and giving me wisdom.

Throughout all of my mistakes, I had my grandparents and art and music to keep me centered. I had a strong core based in my Meskwaki ways. I was conflicted, however, because although my grandparents taught me about being a Meskwaki, I was also living in a world that contradicted those values and beliefs, and I found myself down a dark path that I'm only now making my way out of.

I don't wish to speak of my home or my family in a negative way. I only speak of my life and how I see it, for I love my people and community to the utmost. I would do anything for them and wish to represent them in a positive way. I am still a work in progress, always on a quest for knowledge and working at being a good person every day. As I write this, I have five years of sobriety, going on six, and work with AA to maintain that sobriety.

I hope I can uplift and inspire that Native kid who might feel his life is worthless because he made a bad decision. I hope I can show him that he can change his life and turn it around if he really wants to. In these few stories, I try to explain that I know how easy it can be to slip into bad things. We might believe there is no hope for us when the future is uncertain. I used to think negatively about myself and the world. I was conflicted between the love and teaching of my grandparents, who instilled the Meskwaki values, culture, and traditions in me, and the emotions that come with being a young person in today's world, dealing with adult issues, growing up with absentee parents, seeing and experiencing violence, being around drugs and alcohol, living between two worlds.

I know what it's like to not have anyone encouraging you to do the right thing, disciplining you, providing boundaries. I had my grandparents and uncles, but I didn't have that close parental bond. Like many young Native people, I felt I had to figure things out for myself. I know that feeling of abandonment for the casino, or the bar, or a new relationship, or incarceration, and I know what it is to repeat that pattern as an adult. I know how it feels to think about taking your own life and how it feels to be lost, like you have no place on this Earth. I know how it feels when the world seems against you and the only way out you can see is substance abuse.

We are told not to talk about our feelings and not to express our feelings as boys and men, but I've come to believe that is false. Trying to grow up fast and live fast may seem like fun and games, but the truth of the matter is, it takes us out of the game.

Look at what is happening to our land and our communities. They are being destroyed right under our noses. How can we fight and defend our land if we are constantly intoxicated? How can we see through the smoke screens and fight for our communities when we're drunks, which usually means we have a criminal record, which means we are targeted and marked, which takes away hope and leads us to stay within that cycle? While we are distracted, the system keeps kicking up dust, and in our attempts to clear it, we make it worse.

But that's why we have our eagle fans, to clear dust and smoke. Meaning, pray. Honor our ancestors' teachings. The ancestors are there for us; we just have to talk to them. So, keep the faith. Keep being curious about who we were and who we are. Learn our way of life—our values, our traditions and culture, and most importantly our language, if you have the chance. Regenerate what we have and who we are at our core, and keep that alive.

You also have to find something in this life to keep you sane. For me it was the arts, hip-hop, and all the other cultures and influences that I related to. When I discovered my drawing skills sitting at my desk, or when I found my groove as a grass dancer, or when I first heard Wu-Tang Clan, or when I created a clothing line, I knew that was the world that I belonged in. It was me.

Find a positive outlet and buy yourself some time, because things can get better. You just have to be willing to draw a better world for yourself. You have to forget what people think. You don't have to live up to anyone else's standard or prove anything to anyone.

Times are changing again for us and for the world, so we have to prepare by relearning our ways—the plants, the food systems, the stories, the songs. We can no longer allow distractions like alcohol and drugs to keep us down and afraid. We need to redirect those energies into building up our communities. Replanting our important medicines and foods, our trees and grasses. Relearning our songs and dances, and most importantly, our language, the key to it all.

We don't have a future tense in our language. You can't talk about things that haven't happened yet. It's present and past. When I told people I wanted to go to school, they said, then do it. Don't talk about it. You want to do a thing, then go do it. That's how we are. It's either what have you done already or what you are doing now. That's what my grandparents instilled in me.

We don't anticipate the future because we aren't promised it, but hopefully I'll be here tomorrow to tell you the rest of this story. We Meskwaki, we believe in a balance. There is life and there is death. There is spring and there is fall. And that's how I'm starting to see my own life shape out. I've been on the teeter-totter trying to find my balance. Maybe where I'm existing today is the way to keep the balance. A balance between two worlds: the white man's world and the Native world.

As for me, my grandmother, and my family, we are still here, Red Earth People, people of the Thunder Clan, rumbling across the sky like a storm on the horizon, with rain beaming down the orangish-pink front and little flashes sprinkling along the darker end. Black thunder heard by all those on the Earth.

A NOTE ON THE MESKWAKI LANGUAGE

MESKWAKI IS AN ORAL LANGUAGE. The written language is newly developed, a result both of linguists' attempts to document the language and also, in later years, by tribal elders to preserve it for future generations. The quality of written accuracy is still widely debated—the foundations of the language are completely different than those of European languages, making it incredibly difficult to translate into English. In absence of a translation, the author and editing team decided the best way to honor the language was to share the history of its oral roots.

GLOSSARY | RIVERA

1.5-generation Mexican—Mexican national who migrates to the United States before reaching adulthood. The cutoff age of maturity is around sixteen years of age but varies from study to study. People of the 1.5 generation emigrate before they have reached maturity, which means before their ideals, identity, and nationalism have fully developed. *Note:* The study of generations is not exclusive to Mexicans. You can substitute the word *Mexican* for other nationalities. Also, there are .5 and .75 generations in between, but the definitions are more complicated and vary from researcher to researcher.

advance parole—Temporary travel authorization allowing non-permanent residents to reenter the U.S. after international travel.

agua fresca—Drink made from fruit blended with water, sugar, and lime juice.

amnesty—Pardon. This term was dropped from the rhetoric of immigration rights organizations after anti-immigrant sentiment exploded post-9/11. Before 9/11, organizations fought for legislation similar to the amnesty signed into law in 1986, where undocumented immigrants did not have to learn English or have conditional status before they could become legal permanent residents.

Bracero Program—U.S. program inviting Mexicans to come as seasonal workers, or *braceros*, between 1942 and 1964. It was created to support production and agriculture, keeping the country fed and farms in business while American men were away at war or at work.

comprehensive immigration reform (CIR)—Compromise seen as more likely to become a law than any bill focused on amnesty; mostly comprises enforcement of immigration law and border enforcement with strict guidelines that can legalize some undocumented immigrants after decades of probation, not taking into consideration the time they have lived in the United States without legal status.

Deferred Action for Childhood Arrivals (DACA)—Change in U.S. immigration policy that allowed 1.5-generation immigrants to apply for two-year renewable relief from deportation and a work permit. It is not a law but an executive order. DACA recipients have legal presence but no legal status.

downward assimilation, downward mobility—For immigrants in the U.S. and their descendants, this means acculturating into the dominant underdog culture. For example, their culture, values, and behaviors resemble those of the working class, school-to-prison pipeline, ethnic enclaves, gangs, and slave descendants. The result of downward assimilation can be downward mobility, where there is a loss or stall of generational wealth.

Distrito Federal (D.F.)—Federal District, formerly known as Tenochtitlan, now known as Mexico City. Founded by indigenous people on March 25, 1325, it is where the Mexican federal government is located. In 2016, it was renamed Ciudad de México (CDMX), and its government now has autonomous rule similar to that of a state, but it is not a state. It is a heavily populated city with high GDP, extreme poverty, and extreme wealth.

DREAM Act—Legislation created to address the needs of the 1.5 generation; not currently a law. The needs addressed are access to education and a pathway to citizenship. The first version was introduced by Luis A. Gutierrez, House Representative of Illinois, in 2001 as the Immigrant Children's Educational Advancement and Dropout Prevention Act of 2001. More restrictive and punitive legislation was later introduced as the Student Adjustment Act of 2001 in the House and as the Development, Relief, and Education for Alien Minors (DREAM) Act in the Senate in 2001. People who would qualify for legal status under the act are known as Dreamers.

federal immigration law (basics)—In the United States, the House of Representatives and the Senate have to both pass and agree on a version of a law. Then it is sent to the president to be signed into law. The president has the power to veto it.

first-generation Mexican—Mexican national who migrates to the United States as an adult. Usually has defined ideals, identity, and nationalism by the time of migration.

ICE—Immigration and Customs Enforcement; U.S. federal agency tasked with enforcing immigration laws.

immigration policy—In the United States, the administration of the executive branch can change or implement policies.

INS—Immigration Naturalization Services. Formerly the main federal agency at the border, in 2003 it was split into U.S. Citizenship and Immigration Services (USCIS), Customs and Border Protection (CBP), and Immigration and Customs Enforcement (ICE).

la migra—Spanish term for people who work for INS (later ICE).

matanzas—Slaughterhouses for pigs.

Matrícula Consular—ID given to Mexican nationals who live abroad; often the only ID card that undocumented immigrants from Mexico carry.

mole—Mexican sauce made of chiles and chocolate.

nopal—Cactus in Mexico, included on the flag. To have a nopal on your forehead means you are authentically Mexican.

Oaxaca—Huaxyacac; a state in the southeastern part of Mexico that has a large indigenous population.

pastel—Cake.

pollero—Coyote, the man or woman who took you across the border. After the Clinton announcement of the border wall being built, the business of the border and the cost of these services went up.

pozole—Traditional Mexican soup or stew made with hominy.

remesas—Remittance, or money sent to family members in the home country.

second-generation Mexican American—A U.S.-born child with Mexican parents.

third-generation Mexican American—A U.S.-born child with Mexican grandparents.

tierra—Land.

upward assimilation and upward mobility—For immigrants and their descendants, this means acculturating into the well-off white culture. This can be achieved by getting an education, moving into predominantly white neighborhoods, and being able to blend in.

In the Des Moines area, many immigrants and their descendants experiencing upward assimilation live in West Des Moines, Waukee, and Ankeny.

United Mexican States (Mexico)—Country ruled by indigenous people for thousands of years that was colonized by Spain in the 1500s. It declared its independence from Spain in 1810. In 1848, it ceded one-third of its territory to the United States of America.

zapatos de charol—Patent leather shoes.

GLOSSARY | DIZDAREVIĆ

babo—Bosnian Muslim word for "dad."

BCS—Acronym for Bosnian-Croatian-Serbian; these are dialects of the same language previously referred to as Serbo-Croatian.

Drina river—River that serves as the border between Bosnia and Serbia; throughout history, it has been a symbol of power; the blood of victims from many wars has run through its waters.

Josip Broz Tito—Depending on who you ask, the greatest man to have ever existed or a benevolent dictator; leader of the Yugoslav Partisan resistance; president of the Socialist Federal Republic of Yugoslavia; one of the founders of the Non-Aligned Movement during the Cold War.

rakija—Alcoholic drink made from fermented fruit such as plums, pears, apples, and cherries; it typically has an ABV of 40 to 60 percent.

sin—Bosnian word for "son."

soaking socks in *rakija*—Tradition in the Balkans when a child has a fever; it is believed that if their socks are drenched in rakija and then put on their feet, it will lower body temperature and cure the fever.

šta da vam kažem—Bosnian for "What can I tell you," as in, "What more is there to say."

Socialist Federal Republic of Yugoslavia—Multiethnic southeastern European country that existed for almost thirty years before dissolving into civil war; the countries making up former Yugoslavia include Bosnia and Herzegovina, Croatia, Serbia, Slovenia, Macedonia, Montenegro, and Kosovo.

yugonostalgia—Nostalgic and generally positive feelings that former inhabitants of Yugoslavia feel toward the nation and its leader, Josip Broz Tito; those born outside of Yugoslavia's life span, particularly ethnic Yugoslavs born in the diaspora, may also experience yugonostalgia by means of inherited memory and trauma.

GLOSSARY | PHAM

boat people—Term for the approximately 800,000 refugees who fled Vietnam by boat and ship following the end of the Vietnam War in 1975. The migration was at its peak from 1978 to 1979 but continued throughout the early 1990s. Many Vietnamese died during the passage due to lack of food, overcrowdedness, pirates, and storms. The boat people's first destinations were Hong Kong, Indonesia, Malaysia, the Philippines, Singapore, and Thailand.

C-section—Also known as cesarean delivery; major surgical procedure in which an infant is delivered through an incision in the mother's abdomen and uterus rather than through the vagina.

diaspora—A large group of people with a similar heritage or homeland who have since moved to places all over the world; comes from an ancient Greek word meaning "to scatter about."

Di Sau ("[Maternal] Aunt Six")—Kinship and ranking term referring to my mother's sister, who is the fifth sibling but is ranked sixth because parents are considered number one (hence the counting starts at "two" for the eldest child). Vietnamese language has a complex system of kinship terminology that clearly defines familial hierarchy and the relationship each family member has to each other.

immigrant—Person who comes to one country from another country to take up permanent residence.

kinship terms—Words used to refer to an individual's relations through kinship. Some languages distinguish between maternal and paternal family members, as well as the age of the person. In some communities, terms can even be used for non-kin. Following are some Vietnamese kinship terms:

    cha; bố; ba—father

    mẹ; má—mother

    anh—older brother

    em—younger brother or younger sister

chi—older sister

bác (trai)—elder brother of parents

chú—father's younger brother

cậu—mother's brother

dượng—mother's younger sister's husband

bác (gái)—elder sister of parents

cô—father's younger sister

dì—mother's younger sister

thím—father's younger brother's wife

mợ—mother's brother's wife

anh họ—older male cousin

chị họ—older female cousin

em họ—younger cousin

cháu trai—nephew

cháu gái—niece

ông nội—(paternal) grandfather

ông ngoại—(maternal) grandfather

bà nội—(paternal) grandmother

bà ngoại—(maternal) grandmother

cháu trai—grandson

chau gai—granddaughter

refugee—Person who has been forced to leave their country in order to escape violence, war, persecution, or natural disaster.

refugee resettlement—Process of relocating refugees from an asylum country to another state that has agreed to admit and ultimately grant them permanent settlement.

salted fish—Fish cured with dry salt for preservation. In Vietnam, there are dozens of varieties of salted fish, such as anchovy, sac fish, linh fish, snakehead, anabas, and so on. Salted fish can be eaten as is or may require an additional step of frying in oil.

Vietnam—Long, S-shaped country bordered by China to the north, Laos and Cambodia to the west, and the South China Sea to the east. Vietnamese history is marked by war, colonization, and rebellion.

Vietnamese American—There are 4.5 million Vietnamese living outside of Vietnam in a diaspora. According to the Migration Policy Institute, more than 1.3 million Vietnamese resided in the United States in 2017, accounting for 3 percent of the nation's 44.5 million immigrants and representing the sixth-largest foreign-born group in the country.

GLOSSARY | ELGATIAN

Armenia—Small country in the Middle East that borders Turkey, Iran, Azerbaijan, and Georgia. In the early twentieth century, the Ottomans committed genocide against the Armenian population. The Ottoman Empire is now called Turkey, and the genocide is a source of great controversy for the Turks. Armenia is considered the oldest Christian nation in the world and is one of the first three civilizations to have a written language. Armenia became part of the Soviet Union around World War II.

assimilation—What I mean here is "cultural assimilation," which is when someone from a minority culture takes on the habits and traditions of the dominant culture.

century-long joke—What I'm referring to here is that Mount Ararat is within Turkey's borders, as it has been for the 104 years since the genocide. (The genocide is accepted to have happened in 1915, though it started just before 1900.)

diaspora—A people displaced from their ancestral lands.

fortunes in coffee grounds—You've heard of reading fortunes in tea leaves, right? We drink demitasse cups of thick coffee with the grounds in it, and when the grounds settle, we read fortunes from the shapes.

genocide—This term for deliberate massacres of a particular group of people was invented in response to the mass killings of Armenians by the Ottomans. Some lazy etymology shows "cide" (to kill) combined with "gen" (generation or race).

mail-order marriage—Women in developing countries were listed in catalogs for purchase by men in developed nations. When the women arrived, they would marry. I'm not going to explain how many ways that could go badly.

the mountain/Mount Ararat—Mount Ararat, sometimes referred to as "the mountain," is actually two peaks: Little Ararat and Big Ararat. This is the spiritual and historical center of Armenian culture. It sits just beyond Armenia's border in Turkey.

Near East—Old term for what we now call the Middle East. The Far East is what we usually refer to as Asia.

pilaf—Spiced rice dish.

whiteness—I'm talking about color, here. I'm talking about race. And I'm also talking about the dominant culture in the U.S. Race is based on skin color. When I say "whiteness," I mean that I am literally paler than my father. I also mean that I am closer to the dominant culture than my father is.

Zarouhi—Pronounced zah-rr-ah-wee, this is what my grandmother called me. Sarah becomes "Zara" (remember, we're rolling the "r"), and then the "wee" is added like we add "y" sounds to the ends of things. Zarouhi is also kind of a nickname for Arzarouhi, which is equivalent to Isabelle.

GLOSSARY | HEWEZI

adhan—Muslim call to prayer.

Alhamdulelah—Praise be to *Allah*; all praise is due to God alone; all the praises and thanks be to *Allah*; all praise is due to *Allah*. Said both in times of thankfulness and in times of hardship, this expression is meant to represent the commitment of a Muslim's faith in God, regardless of the circumstances, and demonstrates the belief that God solely acts out of mercy and good will.

Allah—God, the supreme being, infinitely benevolent and powerful, creator of this life and the hereafter; also called *rabena*.

Baba—Father.

basbousa—Semolina cake soaked in sweet syrup, a common Egyptian dessert.

dam—Blood.

dumueh—Tear.

Imshee gam bel heta—Walk alongside the wall. This is an expression often employed to steer people away from the spotlight and *nazar's* evil grip. Individuals who are well-behaved are expected to remain unseen so as not to gain unwanted attention.

Issam—Saint, protector.

Jenna—Heaven, the ultimate goal for any Muslim.

Mama—Mother.

Masha Allah—God has willed. This is a common saying for expressing appreciation, happiness, thankfulness, and recognition for an event, act, or individual.

Noha—Arabic name for females; brain.

nazar—Evil eye; included in the Quran, or Islam's sacred text; the idea that one who is envious of another may cause him bad fortune through his hateful gaze. Muslims seek protection in various ways: saying *Masha Allah*, wearing jewelry or home decor of the blue eye, and reciting the last two *surahs* in the Quran, Al Falaq and Al Nas.

Rana—Arabic name for females; eye-catching, to gaze at longingly.

Reem—Arabic name for females; a white gazelle.

GLOSSARY | MIELKE

abuela—Spanish for "grandma." In my family, the name given to my Great-Grandma Isabel. *Abuela* was my Grandma Margarita's godmother but raised her after her mother died.

devout Catholic—Person who subscribes to very traditional Catholic teachings. In my family, this was expressed by regular attendance at mass, frequent prayer at home, religious imagery in the home, and strong moral convictions.

emerging self—Process of self-discovery. The term implies an experience of bringing conscious awareness to aspects of the self that are already present but unacknowledged.

family script—Set of guidelines that inform how a family defines itself. The influence of a family script affects each member of the family. The family script allows and prohibits the expression of certain thoughts, feelings, and behaviors within the family.

grandparents' couch—The couch in my grandparents' house was a special place for me as a child. I have beautiful memories of being on that couch. I remember lying on my grandpa's chest while he dozed, watching the evening news. And I remember sitting next to my grandma while she read books or watched a cartoon with me. Their home was a safe, secure, loving space for me. I think seeing my dad holding me on my grandparents' couch brought a level of intrigue and curiosity for me.

great things—Refers to the fulfillment of the expectations and beliefs about success that were allowed in my family script. These included a financially lucrative career, getting married and having children, and holiness.

internalized shame—Feeling of unworthiness or worthlessness due to who you are as a person. This attitude is most often adopted by children when shame is a central feature of their life.

origin story—The story of how my mom and dad met, got pregnant, and separated. This term also encapsulates the racial, social, and cultural dynamics that were part of my early life.

political conservative—Person who endorses political values and beliefs that give rise to an emphasis on personal responsibility, aversion to government intervention, and capitalism.

rural Minnesota—Communities in Minnesota that are far from any metropolitan area. These communities largely consist of small towns and agriculture. My mother's family is embedded in the small town in which I was raised. My great-great-grandfather was the first mayor of the town, my great-grandfather was a prominent business owner, my grandfather was the fire chief for twenty-five years, and my mom was the music teacher for several years. As a result, my family lives a very public life in the community. I believe this embeddedness was influential in the suppression of my identity as a Latino.

scandal—In the Catholic Church, scandal is understood as an action or attitude that could cause another person to sin. As used in this story, the acceptance and support of a mother who had a son outside of marriage on the part of the church is referred to as scandal. In the Catholic Church, having a child outside of marriage is considered a serious sin. So, from the perspective of the church community, the avoidance of scandal was necessary in order to promote the good of the church.

shame—Self-perception that one is unworthy of acceptance or love because of who one is *as a person.* The experience of shame is an isolating phenomenon, as it involves a feeling of unworthiness or exclusion. The avoidance of shame can be a powerful driving force in a person's behavior.

social conservative—Person who endorses traditional beliefs regarding morality. These include the belief that marriage is between a man and a woman, sex should only be had by a married man and woman, homosexual relationships are harmful, and abortion and euthanasia are harmful. These beliefs are often informed by traditional religious values.

suppression—Dealing with thoughts, feelings, and experiences by avoiding or denying them. Suppression often leads to harmful consequences for individuals and families.

GLOSSARY | DAVENPORT

blood quantum—Federal laws try to define Native membership in tribes based on biological ancestry. We Natives believe that if you have any of our blood in you, you are part of us, but the blood quantum system says you must have a certain percentage to be recognized.

bone dice—Game involving a wooden bowl with pieces carved out of bone. There is a turtle and a bear, and the object is to stand up the bear. If you want in on a round, you throw a penny in a dish. The person who stands up the bear, or gets the most points that round, gets the bowl of pennies.

clan—Familial group responsible for a specific area in the tribe. Meskwakis are born into a clan system based on paternity.

commods—Commodities, or food given to Native communities by the government. The food consisted of canned meats, powdered milk, large tubs of peanut butter, and the infamous large block of cheese. This food was given as rations for the poverty we endured and for the loss of our traditional food systems.

head roach—Headpiece made from porcupine quills, once worn by great Meskwaki warriors to taunt enemies, then as decorative pieces, and today worn at powwows.

Indian Relocation Act—In 1956, the federal government passed the Indian Relocation Act in an attempt to encourage Native Americans to leave their reservations and assimilate into urban areas. My grandparents moved around the country for a few years as a result of the act but found the promises of a better life were false, and they eventually returned to the Settlement to raise their family.

Indian Removal Act—In 1830, the federal government passed the Indian Removal Act to forcibly relocate thousands of Native Americans. In the late 1800s, the government began another round of assimilation tactics, removing Native children from their homes and sending them to boarding schools.

Indian Residential Schools—Boarding schools that were designed to assimilate Native children into white society. Often if students

197

spoke of their Native life or in their Native language, they were punished or beaten. Today many schools have been turned into all-Indian schools that Native students attend from all over the country. For me, it was a combination of a trade school and a standard high school; I learned auto-body work while going to regular high school classes.

Institute of American Indian Arts (IAIA)—College in Santa Fe that focuses on Native arts and culture. My mom studied creative writing there, and I visited her with my grandparents once when I was a kid. Her education there helped inspire me in my own pursuit of the arts.

Jordans—Shoes from Nike's Air Jordan line, originally designed for Michael Jordan of the Chicago Bulls.

kekyaaki—Old ones or old people (pronounced *keh-gyah-hah-gi*).

Meskwaki—Red Earth People, a Native people who lived in North America long before the European settlers came, roaming free and caring for the land.

meskwi—Blood (pronounced *mesh-kwi*); also the word in Meskwaki for the color red.

otenikani—Summerhouse; outside cooking shack; place used for cooking for large family gatherings. Similar to a shelter at a park. A place where we get together as a family and enjoy each other's presence.

powwow—Native cultural event with singing, dancing, and celebration. The Meskwaki annual powwow has existed for over a hundred years. It began as a religious dance celebrating a good harvest and giving thanks to the Creator for all we have. I traveled to powwows around the region with my grandparents, who owned a snow cone and cotton candy stand, and I danced as a fancy dancer and am still a grass dancer.

the Settlement—Meskwaki land in Tama County, Iowa; also known as the Sett for short. Around 1847, the Meskwaki worked out an agreement with a local farmer and the governor to establish the Settlement. It is a settlement rather than a reservation because we bought our land.

Thunder Clan (Wemiko)—Clan that is responsible for peace, interpreting on behalf of the tribe, and taking care of everything associated with storms. My Thunder Clan name is Makatenenemekiwa, which means "Black Thunder."

tobacco—Sacrament used as an offering by the Meskwaki to pray to their Creator.

CONTRIBUTORS

MIRIAM ALARCON AVILA

DAWSON DAVENPORT is a member of the Meskwaki Nation and grew up on the Meskwaki Settlement near Tama, Iowa, where he was raised by his maternal grandparents. He tells stories about his experiences as a Native, both the challenges he has faced and the Meskwaki way of life. He graduated from the University of Iowa with a degree in art and a certificate in entrepreneurial management. He spends his time in Iowa City and on the Meskwaki Settlement as an entrepreneur, doing graphic design; running his clothing brand, Daepian Apparel; and opening a Native arts gallery in Iowa City.

MIRIAM ALARCON AVILA

AJLA DIZDAREVIĆ is a Bosnian American who grew up in Waterloo, Iowa. Her writing concerns itself with the Balkan experience and post-war diaspora life. A student at the University of Iowa majoring in English and creative writing, she has won the Iowa Chapbook Prize and the David Hamilton Undergraduate Creative Writing Prize. She is also a recipient of the Iowa Scholarship for the Arts from the Iowa Department of Cultural Affairs. She hopes to share underrepresented narratives not only through her own work but also through others' writing with the Slavic diaspora magazine *Gastarbajter.*

SARAH ELGATIAN is a second-generation Armenian American with a lot of questions. Her paternal grandparents came to the United States through Ellis Island, barely escaping the Armenian genocide. She was born and raised in the Quad Cities and later moved to Chicago and Seattle before returning to Iowa. As a writer, she primarily writes nonfiction and lyrical essays focusing on survival. Her writing has been published in *Beholder Magazine, Crab Fat,* and more. She lives Iowa City, Iowa, with her partner and works at the Midwest Writing Center and with the International Writing Program.

RANA HEWEZI was born in Cairo, Egypt. When she was two, her family moved to France, and when she was seven, they moved to Ames, Iowa. She writes lyrical nonfiction that confronts and resists the oppression, fear, and ignorance of society. Many of her stories are centered around familial expectations and her culture. She has been published literary magazines such as *Earthwords* and *Teen Ink Magazine,* and she is a winner of the Iowa Chapbook Prize. She currently attends the University of Iowa studying philosophy and English, and she hopes to go to medical school after graduation.

ANTHONY MIELKE was born and raised in Minnesota with his mother, stepfather, and five younger siblings, unaware of his Puerto Rican heritage on his paternal side. He studied philosophy at the University of St. Thomas in St. Paul and then earned his master's and doctorate in family and marriage therapy. Today, after discovering his heritage, he uses writing to explore themes of identity, isolation, spirituality, and healing through an introspective lens. He lives with his wife and three children in Cedar Rapids, Iowa, where he is an assistant professor in marriage and family therapy at Mount Mercy University and practices therapy.

HIEU PHAM was born in Mỹ Tho, Vietnam, but her family sought refuge in the United States when she was three to escape the political persecution and poverty of the area. After spending two years in refugee camps in Malaysia and the Philippines, they were able to settle in Des Moines, Iowa. She enjoys writing about her family and what it's like to be a mother, but she also centers much of her work around the Vietnamese diaspora and Asian-American culture. She lives with her husband and two children in Des Moines, where she works as an advocate for Asian victims of domestic abuse and sexual assault at Monsoon Asian and Pacific Islanders in Solidarity.

MIRIAM ALARCON AVILA

ANTONIA RIVERA was born in Distrito Federal, Mexico. At age six she crossed the border, and she spent her youth in California before moving around the United States as part of immigration organizing movements. Eventually she received temporary protection and a work permit through DACA (Deferred Action for Childhood Arrivals). She writes about migration and what it means to be part of the 1.5 generation. She lives in Des Moines, Iowa, with her daughter and works at Wells Fargo.

EDITORS

ANDREA WILSON is the founder and Executive Director of the Iowa Writers' House, the creator of the Bicultural Iowa Writers' Fellowship, and the series editor of *We the Interwoven*. She grew up in Columbus Junction, a small Iowa farming community experiencing a cultural shift from the meat-packing industry and seasonal agricultural work. In her early adulthood, she lived in Toronto, Canada, and began to write cultural stories. She traveled and lived throughout Latin America before returning to Iowa City and founding the Iowa Writers' House. She is dedicated to working with underrepresented voices and helping them tell their stories.

ALISHA JEDDELOH is the Associate Director of the Iowa Writers' House and assistant editor of the *We the Interwoven* series. She grew up on a farm outside Fairfield, Iowa, home to both cornfields and the golden domes of Maharishi Mahesh Yogi and his university. The culture clash between groups led her to see difference as a catalyst for creativity and new ways of being, and that experience continues to inform her work as a writer and editor today. She lives in Iowa City, Iowa, with her family, where she is currently working on a novel that explores community and belonging.

RESOURCES

The following resources for readers are available at
WWW.WETHEINTERWOVEN.COM

～

TESTIMONIALS AND REVIEWS

We would like to hear from you about your experience as a reader. Tell us what you discovered by reading this book or how it affected you.

DISCUSSION GUIDES

This book was created to start conversations. If you'd like to form a discussion group, we've created free guides that are available at our website.

TELL US YOUR STORY

If you or your family members have a story to share of migration and starting a new life in America, we'd like to hear it. Each fall we take applications for the Bicultural Writers' Fellowship, and in the meantime, we'll be reading the stories people choose to share with us through our website. While we can't publish them all, we want you to know that your story matters, and that the process of writing our stories can be a way of understanding our own place in the human experience.